# Heroes

## 50 Stories *of the* AMERICAN SPIRIT

## Lenore Skomal

This book is dedicated to all those who gave
their lives selflessly on Sept. 11, 2001

# HEROES

Library of Congress Cataloging-in-Publication 200109778

ISBN -13:978-1495244261
ISBN-10:1495244261

Jacket photographs: Flag David Waldorf/FPG/Getty
Images Firefighter Bill Stormont/Corbis
Stock Market Cover design by Whitney Cookman
Book design by Frances J. Soo Ping Chow
Formatting by RikHall.com

# ACKNOWLEDGEMENTS

This is the revised edition of *Heroes: 50 Stories of the American Spirit*, originally published under the Running Press imprint several months after the tragedy of 9/11. Below, is the original acknowledgements section that was printed in the first edition:

A book of this nature takes the cumulative effort of not one but many people. Thanks to the support from all of those who desperately wanted to see it published, Heroes was born and brought into this world quickly but not without great effort.

Quite frankly, there would be no book in front of you, at least not so quickly, without the efforts of many people at Running Press, who put on the full court press to aid me in finding the best fifty stories.

I also extend my gratitude to all those who agreed to be interviewed. Talking about something deeply troubling, especially when feelings are still so raw, is not easy. But with the sharing comes understanding. Thank you for giving that to me and to the reader.

Perhaps most of all, I am deeply indebted to the journalists around the world who worked round the clock to bring the events of September 11th and beyond alive for the rest of us.

While journalism is often a thankless career, and, as a profession, comes under intense criticism, I am very proud to come from its ranks. I deeply thank all of those who diligently worked their craft during that crucial time to leave clear documentation for the generations to come. It is your work that I have drawn on. I can only hope I did it justice. Thanks for your tireless efforts.

# THE NEW PATRIOTISM
## A CALL TO ACTION

Since September 11th, the courageous acts of countless Americans have set a new standard for the nation. As the world watched the horror on television, it also witnessed what is best in our country and our character. As buildings collapsed, the American spirit soared.

The indelible images of the first days will live on in all the days of our history. Firefighters and police risked their lives and gave their lives to save others, and hundreds of rescuers paid the ultimate price. The brave passengers of Flight 93 fought and defied the terrorists, and in the face of their own inevitable deaths, they prevented the killing of so many others.

Construction and health workers went into the shadow of constant danger to search for the missing and help the survivors. The mayor of New York City went everywhere, sustaining the city. New Yorkers lined up for blocks to give blood, and so did thousands more across the country. Hundreds of millions of dollars poured in for the families of the victims, as valiantly, tearfully and quietly they said goodbye to a mother, father, son, daughter or friend in funeral after funeral.

And through it all, Americans began to think deeply about our country again. We got a new sense of the precious nature of our freedom, which, in the years after the Cold War, we have increasingly taken for granted. We have learned anew to prize the experiment called America—a nation based not on sameness, but on diversity—a nation of different races, backgrounds and faiths, defined not by accident of geography or history, but by the high aspirations for a better life and greater opportunity that brought so many millions to these shores from every continent and country on earth.

Now we have seen, perhaps, more clearly than ever before in our lives, how we are all in this together—how, if even one of us is hurting, all of us hurt. Our first thoughts on September 11th were about others, not ourselves.

That spirit must now live on. It is the new standard by which we must measure everything we do. The spirit of September 11th points the way. In that spirit we must continue to care about each other, and fulfill the promise and opportunity of America for all people.

This time called for active citizenship, whether by children getting involved in service learning programs at school or senior citizens signing up for the Retired Senior Volunteer program.

Active citizenship will sustain us in the challenges ahead. We must not reject any attempt to misuse the terrorist threat as an excuse to deny or delay our obligations to teach our children well, to treat the sick, help the needy and make the new economy a new foundation for a stronger family life and a higher standard of living for all our families.

We have heard such excuses for inaction in the past. We will hear them again in this crisis—that the war on terrorism will deplete our resources and delay our commitment to a "more perfect union." But we always kept faith with America's ideals, and came together to respond to the greatest social needs. We mobilized our government and our whole nation, wisely and well, to defeat our enemies and meet the demands of our best ideals.

It has never been more critical to do so than it is today.

If we meet the new standards of September 11th, no one will stand in our way, and many more will join us. And the heroes of that day will have left an undying legacy—a proud new chapter in the annals of America's greatness.

Let us pledge our energies to this cause. Let us show, that as the battle goes on for a world free from fear, the work goes on to move America forward.

—*Senator Edward M. Kennedy*

Oct. 24, 2001

*Excerpted with permission from the "Statement of Senator Edward M. Kennedy on the Economic Stimulus Package," October 24, 2001.*

For the full text, go to

www.senate.gov/-kennedy/statements/0H10/2001A25B49.html

# ABOUT THIS BOOK

When I watched the second plane sail into the side of the Twin Towers, I stood riveted. Over and over again, I watched the clip of that hijacked passenger plane. The moment ripped open an old memory, one neatly tucked away in my mind—one of a 25-year-old radio reporter traveling back from vacation, minding her own business, not unlike much of America on September 11th.

I was on a hijacked plane New Year's Eve in 1984. Flight 626 was returning from the Caribbean when it abruptly changed destination from JFK to Havana, Cuba, without my understanding, without my consent. The terror, the shock and the honest bewilderment that accompanies such a violation is multi-dimensional, and one that I am sure all of those brave souls on the four doomed planes on September 11th could not fully process in the short time they had.

There were 197 others along with me on that American Airlines plane—all ages and colors. When the cold reality sank in that we were being held hostage and now heading to another country, I was furious. In fact, *The New York Times* quoted me as saying, "I got madder and madder and madder. It got to the point where I just wanted to go back and smash the guy. "

It was most likely that type of anger that led the fearless actions of the heroes on Flight 93.

I clearly remember one point on the grueling flight to Cuba, when an icy horror climbed over me, as I took long looks at those strangers sitting around me during our shared four-hour ordeal. A couple sat next to me with their four small children, all boys. The oldest, a ten-year old, looked up to his father and told him, "Dad, don't worry about a thing. But just remember that I love you. I really love you."

Tears filled his father's eyes and mine. A married couple sat across the aisle from me. They held hands and wept silently in the darkness. An elderly man behind me mumbled, softly pushing prayer beads through his cupped hands. A sinking certainty overcame me. I knew in that moment that I would probably die with these people. These would be the last faces I would see during my lifetime.

But I did not die, and for one simple reason. Ishmael Ali Labeet, the madman who took over our plane, had planned to go to Havana. And while he carelessly walked the line between humanity and terror, shaking his handguns frantically at the flight crew one minute and joking with them about their kids the next, the ultimate deciding factor of our destiny was his selfishness. He wanted to live. And one person decided the fate of 198 people.

So when Running Press Book Publishers in Philadelphia approached me to write *Heroes: Fifty Stories of the American Spirit*, there was a certain irony to the assignment. Writing the book proved to be healing for me.

The idea itself came from Buz Teacher, then publisher of Running Press. His vision for this book was clear. It would celebrate the good that came out of the tragedy and the goodness of Americans, particularly the heroism of ordinary people. Hence the challenge to me: produce 50 fully researched and well-written stories in 30 days.

My task was to come up with a broad enough mix to represent the whole— uniformed personnel and civilians, children to senior citizens; New Yorkers to Hawaiians. We wanted to make sure each segment of the population was represented in some way. We were looking for "feel good" stories so that the collection as a whole would make us feel proud about being Americans. That was the criteria we used as we struggled with the questions of which stories to include and who might rightly qualify as a hero.

Chances are, none of the people profiled in this book consider themselves heroes. The accolade is not given lightly. It connotes unusual respect, on par with the terms "saint" or "statesman." The 13 stories in Section 1 are about people who made the ultimate sacrifice, laying down their lives for others. The stories are meant to be representative, rather than all-inclusive. Certainly, there were many, many more who did the same on September 11th. The total number of New York firefighters, paramedics and police officers who were killed in the line of duty that day exceeds 400.

Although we could have filled the pages of this book, and then some, with their awe-inspiring stories, we chose to broaden the book's scope. Our intention: to demonstrate that each and every individual, no matter what his age or profession, is capable of rising to the occasion and serving the greater good. In these pages there a multitude of examples of that. Among them are people like Alayne

Gentul, Bruce Eagleson and Zhe Zeng, each of whom could have gotten themselves home safely that day. But they put the welfare of others ahead of their own, and died a hero's death.

Heroes captures only a smattering of the good that emerged in response to the terrorist attacks. Some small—and not so small— noble deeds are known only to those who perished beneath the rubble at the World Trade Center, at the Pentagon, or in the Somerset County, PA, field where United Flight 93 crashed. Others are recorded only in the hearts of people who benefited from these actions. Recorded or not, every such deed contributes to the collective spirit of America, enriching us all.

Firefighters, police officers, people from the construction trades and others (including some very dedicated and well-trained dogs) looked for human remains at Ground Zero, as they carefully clear the wreckage. The rescue and recovery workers have done so under very hazardous conditions, facing daily what most of us could not bear. Without their collective efforts, their quiet heroism, it would take far longer to complete the work that needed to be done so we could heal and start anew.

We hope you will join us in saluting each and every one of them.

I decided to republish this book under my own imprint when it went out of print because I believe this book is a snapshot of what America went through in the days that followed the horrific acts of terrorism on 9/11. And someday, we will want to have a record of even the smallest of heroic acts that made those days remarkable in their own way.

—*Lenore Skomal*

# Contents

# THE ULTIMATE SACRIFICE

## "OK. LET'S ROLL."

Of all the stories of heroism that emerged on September 11th, none so captured America's heart as the story of the United Airlines Flight 93 passengers who defied the terrorists. These men exemplify the ideal of manhood. Courageous in the face of death, they remained clear-headed amidst the chaos and enough in control of themselves to take effective action. God only knows how many lives they saved on the ground, how many families were spared anguish. Given speculation that the flight was headed to the Capitol, it's possible they helped preserve America's government, preventing the massive loss of lives that would have thrown it into chaos at such a critical time.

As S. Hammer so aptly observed in a letter to *The New York Times*, the individuals on Flight 93 make it clear "that courageous, moral acts are not out of reach for any of us...They provide us with a stirring and inspiring example of what each one of us, working together with loved ones and with fellow citizens, can achieve."

What is so remarkable is that none of the men knew each other, even though Todd Beamer and Mark Bingham graduated from the same California high school. And yet, they were able to quickly reach consensus on a life-death decision using that old standby of democracy—the vote. When you begin to examine their backgrounds and their passions, some similarities emerge. We do know that all but one were Gen-Xers, and all served in managerial roles in their companies. Indeed, Mark Kendall Bingham owned his.

Unfortunately for the terrorists, they were also big guys, many of them athletes who had earned some glory in high school and college, and they stayed active. You see, as much as the terrorists had meticulously planned their suicide missions, they could never have foreseen the problems they'd encounter trying to maintain control on a flight carrying what you have to concede was God's All-Star Team.

Black belt Jeremy Glick had been an all-state wrestler, and in 1993, he had won the national collegiate judo championship in the 220-pound class. Mark Burnett had been Jefferson High School's starting quarterback in the 1980s. Lou Nacke was a power weight lifter, with the muscles to show for it. Todd Beamer had played basketball and baseball for Wheaton College, and was now on his church's softball team. Bingham, a rugby coach and player, had recently returned from Pamplona, Spain, where he ran with the bulls. Years earlier, he had bare-handedly disarmed a thug who threatened him and his friends.

Among them, these passengers on Flight 93 knew how to call a play, tackle, pin, disarm and disable an opponent.

But their sports background alone didn't account for the mental control, the absolute refusal of these men to be paralyzed by fear. Nor does it account for the audacity it must have taken to hatch a takeover plan while terrorists sat among them. Nor did it account for the character that led them to risk their own lives to spare the lives of people they didn't know and would never meet.

To get an inkling of what led them toward that decision, you'd have to look to their lives. Who were these men prior to the morning of Sept. 11, 2001? How had life prepared them for this moment? Was it chance, or destiny, that brought them together?

## Among the Heroes

MARK KENDALL BINGHAM was born May 22, 1970 in Phoenix, he lived for a time in Miami, and then headed out to California with his mother, Alice Hogland. They moved around a bit, living for a time in towns like Riverside, Monterey and Albany. As a 16-year-old student at Los Gatos High School, Bingham discovered his passion for rugby. It would become central to his life. Later, as an international relations major at the University of California at Berkeley, he twice led the school to the national college title in rugby. Friends described him as very competitive, and not a good loser. But he was liked. In fact, he was president of his UC-Berkeley fraternity.

Bingham was masculine to the core, a bit of a rowdy, actually. He was also gay. People who knew him well said it took time for him to reconcile the different sides of himself. Once he did, however, he was determined to become a role model for other gay men. In this capacity, he was instrumental in helping to get the San Francisco Fog, a gay rugby team, off the ground.

The Fog, the first such rugby club in the western United States, was founded to welcome minorities, including men of color, to the sport. Just a few days before September 11th, Bingham was gratified to learn that his team had been accepted as a permanent member of a straight Northern California rugby league.

In an e-mail he sent to his teammates shortly afterwards, he said, "We have a chance to be role models for other gay folks who wanted to play sports but never felt good enough or strong enough. More importantly, we have the chance to show the other teams in the league that we are as good as they are."

Teammate Mike Grant said there was "no one more spirited, on and off the field."

Bingham, 6'5" and 220 pounds, delighted in his physicality. He would not let himself be cowed by anyone or anything. Paul Holm, his former partner of six years, said Bingham's nature was to "protect the weaker." He was with Bingham in San Francisco when a group of men, including one who was armed, confronted Bingham and several friends. They say Bingham leapt out front, knocked the gun out of the attacker's hand, and then pummeled the assailants until they ran. Other friends, who accompanied him to Pamplona, Spain, saw him get up, dust himself off and order a beer after he was thrown down and stomped on by a bull. He was simply irrepressible.

3

He had business savvy, too. After working in public relations for several companies, Bingham founded The Bingham Group, which specialized in high-tech PR. He built it into a bicoastal business, with offices in San Francisco and New York. The reason Bingham found himself on United Airlines Flight 93 that day was twofold.

He had an afternoon meeting with a client in San Francisco. He had planned to fly out the day before, but was too sick from a hangover after attending a friend's birthday party. Sometime prior to 8 a.m. on the morning of September 11th, the 31-year-old Bingham settled into seat 4C on United Airlines Flight 93.

Unbeknownst to him, he sat right behind two of the terrorists.

Seated next to Bingham was Tom Burnett, Jr., the 38-year-old senior vice president and chief executive officer of Thoratec Corp., a Pleasanton, CA, medical device company. Burnett was a big guy, too. He carried 205 pounds on his 6'2" frame.

Burnett was born fighting for life—in this case, his. His mother, Beverly, called him her "miracle baby," because he came after she suffered through a few miscarriages. He barely made it. Born quite prematurely on May 29, 1963, he was so small, his mother said, that his foot was the size of a thumb. He had to be fed constantly; his sucking reflex stimulated each time. Eventually he put on enough weight to thrive.

In the Minneapolis suburbs where he lived with his family, Burnett grew into a hardy child. He loved outdoor activities like fishing with his father, Tom Sr., and he was an avid sportsman. In 1980, he earned a place as the starting quarterback for the Jefferson High School Jaguars in Bloomington, MN. Coach Bruno Walden remembers him as a "super leader...he'd lead by doing." He said Burnett showed a penchant for strategic thinking even then.

Burnett showed enough promise to get him appointed to the Air Force Academy, but he didn't stay long. Deciding that he'd rather give orders than take them, he transferred to another college, ultimately earning his MBA from the Carlson School of Management at the University of Minnesota. He was a member of the university's Alpha Kappa Psi fraternity.

Burnett's career required frequent travel. Deena, his wife of nine years at the time of the hijackings, was a stewardess for Delta Airlines when they met. Despite the amount of time he spent on planes, Burnett never forgot the risks. After the couple had children, he never got on the same flight as his wife because he didn't want his children to lose both parents at once. He had three children back home in San

Ramon who were then 3-year-old Anna Clare and 5-year-old twins Madison and Holly. Friends say they meant everything to him.

Burnett was as devoted to his Catholic faith as he was to his family. He attended mass daily and called upon the Poor Clare Sisters when his family needed prayers. Those who knew him well said he was especially fond of the writings of Thomas Aquinas, Thomas a Kempis and Thomas Merton. He could be eloquent himself. In a speech he gave when another company merged with his, he said, "The struggle ... to preserve life enriches all of us and our humanity is fortified by the process. To deem life important and to act affects all of those who bear witness to it."

Burnett was returning home from a business trip on the morning of September 11th. He was due to go out on a later flight, but switched to Flight 93 so he could get home to his young family earlier.

Louis Nacke, a 5'9," 200-pound distribution center director for Kay-Bee Toys, had just booked the flight the night before. The 42-year-old Nacke rarely traveled but agreed to help a customer in Sacramento with inventory problems. The New Hope, PA, father of two had married Amy Trichon in September 2000, after a long stretch as a single man. He had two sons from a previous relationship, Joseph, 18, and Louis, 14 at the time of 9/11 attacks.

Friends said he had a taste for fine wines and cigars. But stuffy he was not. Nacke liked his music loud. He was a Pittsburgh Steelers fan. He was a power-lifter, who sported a red and yellow Superman logo tattoo on his left arm. He was also sentimental. In his wallet he carried a laminated piece of napkin, decorated by Joseph, who at the time was 6.

Besides his sons, Nacke's other pride and joy was his red Corvette. He loved to edge past other people on the road, radio blasting, until Amy talked him into selling the sportster so they could save more money for the house they planned to buy. Nacke agreed, but the proceeds from the sale never made it into the bank. Instead, he used them to buy his wife diamond earrings. They were to celebrate their first anniversary Sept. 16.

Jeremy Glick, 31, was a sales manager for Vividence, a San Mateo, CA, Internet company. As a young boy—one, perhaps who had an inkling of his destiny—he was smitten with superheroes. He would sometimes call his sister "Wonder Woman" instead of Jennifer, and his own nickname was "Green Lantern," after the comic book superhero who made his home in a crater. That's curious, given that Flight 93 carved a crater out of the earth on impact.

Glick was one of six children born to Lloyd and Joan Glick. Like many Jewish parents, they believed so strongly in the importance of a good education that they sent their entire brood to the elite Upper Saddle River Day School in northern New Jersey. Friends remember how hard they worked to afford the expense. The school wasn't far from the family home in Oradell.

At Upper Saddle River Day School, Glick was active in sports. He was an all-state wrestler, played lacrosse and was captain of the soccer team. His soccer coach, Joe Augineillo, remembers him as a "tough, hard-nosed kid." No doubt, some of the discipline he applied to those sports came from his study of judo. He was only 7 when he began training under Sensei Nagaysu Ogasawara at the Kokushi dojo in Westwood, NJ.

Ogasawara's own daughter, Liliko, was a U.S. Olympian. He worked to build character as well as proficiency in his students. Glick kept progressing, soon earning his black belt. At age 15, he nearly won a national junior championship.

When he left New Jersey to major in English at the University of Rochester, Glick continued to compete in judo events. In 1993, he was named the U.S. national collegiate champion in the 220-pound class. The fact that the university had no judo team and no coach didn't deter him. He coached himself. Ogasawara remembers him as being not just physically strong, but mentally, too.

Yet, he was also known for his sweetness and gentle sense of humor. Glick met his wife, Lyz, in a ninth-grade biology class at Upper Saddle River Day School. They were such a popular couple that high school classmates elected them Prom King and Queen back in 1988. In August 2001, they celebrated their fifth anniversary. That year, they also had their first child, a daughter, Emerson, who was born earlier than expected.

Glick's wife, Lyz, said the only time she ever saw her husband cry was the day his daughter was born. Emmie was just 12 weeks old when Glick's company asked him to come to California for a business meeting. He felt extreme reluctance to leave them. Lyz said she urged him to go. Glick planned to take a flight out Sept. 10, but traffic to the airport was so heavy, he missed it. That's how 6'2" strong-minded judo champion ended up on Flight 93 on September 11th.

Todd Beamer, 32, of Cranbury, NJ, was an account manager for Oracle Corporation. Born in Flint, MI, he was the only son of David and Peggy Beamer. The couple also had two daughters, Michelle and Melissa.

Beamer attended Wheaton Christian Grammar School and Wheaton Academy in Illinois. After the family moved to Los Gatos, CA in 1986, Todd began his senior year at Los Gatos High School, the very same high school Mark Bingham attended. During his year there, Beamer played varsity basketball and baseball.

After high school, Beamer returned to Illinois to major in business administration at Wheaton College. He went on to receive his master's degree in business administration from DePaul University in 1993.

Beamer's friends describe him as kind and gracious. His sixth-grade teacher, Steve Johnson, was so impressed with his integrity that he hired him for his computer business after Beamer graduated from college. Oracle hired him seven years ago.

Beamer's faith was very important to him. A member of the Princeton Alliance Church in Plainsboro, NJ, Beamer had served as a youth mentor and sponsor since the mid-1990s. He also taught senior high school Christian Education classes for several years.

He was a family man, too. Beamer married another Wheaton alumnus. He started dating Lisa a few years after he graduated. After marrying, the couple moved to New Jersey, where they both had positions with Oracle. They had two sons, David Paul and Andrew Todd, and were expecting a third in January 2002.

Like so many others on Flight 93, Todd Beamer was headed west for a business meeting. And like Bingham and Glick, he originally planned to fly out Sept. 10. He decided to spend that evening at home with his pregnant wife and young sons, and fly out early the next morning.

There may have been others. Among the passengers was Richard Guadagno, 38, a refuge manager for U.S. Fish and Wildlife Services who had federal law enforcement training. Flight attendant CeCee Lyles, 34, had been a police officer for six years before changing to her current career. Donald Greene, 52, was the chief executive officer for Safe Flight Instrument Corp.

Unfortunately, all we have to go on are the accounts by family members who received those last, desperate calls. Those who did not reach their families left no record of their last actions.

## The Drama Unfolds

UNITED FLIGHT 93 took off from Newark Airport about 40 minutes behind schedule, at 8:44 a.m. The 757 jet was carrying a light load—38 passengers, five flight attendants and two pilots. (The plane seated 182.) Everything went as planned for close to an hour. Flight attendants served breakfast. Apparently there was no sign anything was amiss until the plane reached Cleveland.

On the ground, however, news that two planes had crashed into the World Trade Towers just minutes after Flight 93 left the ground had spread over the airwaves. Lyzbeth Glick was visiting her parents' home in New York's Catskill Mountains. Baby Emmie had kept her up all night, so she missed her husband's 7:30 a.m. pre-flight call. But she was awake when her brother called from Westchester to tell his folks to turn on the TV. Lyzbeth's father, Richard Macklin, knew his son-in-law was in the air. He turned the televisions off because he didn't want his daughter to worry.

Across the country in Saratoga, CA, Mark Bingham's mother, Alice Hogland, was still asleep at her brother's home.

Deena Burnett was in her Sam Ramon, CA, kitchen, fixing breakfast for her three young daughters. She had the television on. She knew her husband planned to fly home from the New York area that morning but didn't know his flight number. His mother, Beverly, also knew her son was flying home from the East Coast, since Tom Burnett had called her that morning from his New York hotel room. Beverly had heard about the problems in New York and called Deena from the family home in Minnesota.

The terrorists must have sprung into action around 9:30. At least two were seated in first class, in front of Mark Bingham and Tom Burnett. Brandishing their box cutters, the terrorists stabbed one passenger to death and forced their way into the cockpit, ousting the pilot and copilot. (It is not clear from passenger accounts whether they wounded or murdered them, too.) Cleveland air traffic controls picked up a radio transmission from Flight 93 in which they heard an American voice screaming "Get out of here. Get out of here." And then silence. They presume that the man screaming was the pilot.

Two hijackers locked themselves into the cockpit. A third, who claimed that the box he had strapped around his waist was a bomb, herded 27 of the passengers into the first-class compartment near the front of the plane. He ordered another 10 passengers and the flight attendants to sit on the floor in the galley at the rear of the 757s cabin.

At 9:38 a.m., the plane made a hairpin turn and headed toward Washington, DC. Controllers next heard a transmission from a man with a foreign accent, who identified himself as the captain. He said there was a bomb on board, and they were returning to the airport. He spoke into the cockpit microphone, instead of the public address system so it's likely that passengers never heard him. In Washington, DC, a minute later, Flight 77 slammed into the Pentagon.

Jeff Krawcyzk, chief executive of Flight Explorer, a software firm that uses the Federal Aviation Administration to track flights, said that Flight 93 took several sharp turns, all within about two or three minutes.

"It was going west, then north, and then west again." The plane headed toward Kentucky, then took a short turn toward DC, he said. It was just about then that the FAA center in Cleveland lost contact with the flight. Someone apparently shut off its transponder. One of the hijackers did file a new flight plan, however, showing that the plane was on a direct course to Washington, DC.

The plane took a few more erratic turns, which led the FAA to contact the municipal airport in Johnstown, PA, warning officials there to evacuate the tower because of a suspicious plane.

Deena was still talking to her mother-in-law when she picked up her husbands phone call via call waiting. She immediately asked Tom whether he was OK.

"No," he said. "I'm on the airplane, United Flight 93, and it's been hijacked." He told her that the hijackers had knifed a guy and had a bomb on board. 'Please call the authorities,'" he said, and hung up. Deena called 911 immediately.

Todd Beamer tried to call his wife on the Airfone, but his credit card was rejected. When the GTE operator established that he was on a hijacked plane, she transferred the call to supervisor Lisa Jefferson. A log shows that the call was patched through at around 9:45. Beamer told Jefferson that he had been among 10 passengers ordered to sit in the back of the plane. She told him about the other hijackings. Their conversation was to last approximately 13 minutes.

Glick, who was also ordered to the back of the plane, called his wife from the Airfone at about 9:45. His father-in-law, Richard Macklin, picked up. "There's bad men on the plane," said Glick. "Let me talk to Lyz." Lyz's mother had the presence of mind to call 911 from a separate phone so authorities could patch into the line. The family provided information to state police in New York.

Jeremy and Lyz spent more than 20 minutes on the phone assuring each other of their love, and exchanging information. He had heard from other passengers that other hijacked planes had crashed into the World Trade Center and wanted to know if that was true. Lyz told him, "You need to be strong, but yes, they are doing that." He was trying to figure out whether the terrorists planned to blow up the plane or use it as yet another guided missile.

He also told Lyz how much he loved his daughter, Emerson, and asked her to take care of her. Then he told Lyz: "Whatever decisions you make in your life, I need you to be happy, and I will respect any decisions that you make." Lyz said he sounded strong and clear-headed.

Deena was talking with the FBI when Tom called again with an update. He asked her about the World Trade Center. He wanted to know whether the hijackers had used a passenger airline. Deena said she didn't know. He said, "OK, I have to go." She told NBC's *Dateline* that "his adrenaline was flowing. He was trying to sort it out. I think he realized much sooner than I did that it was a suicide."

It's not clear how or exactly when the men talked over their options and took a vote. But Tom called Deena less than a minute after he had hung up. They talked about whether the bomb was real or phony. Burnett thought the hijackers were bluffing. He was also clear that they couldn't wait for the authorities to do something. The men on board had to act by rushing the terrorists, he said. He told her "there's a group of us and we're going to do something."

"No," she said, hoping to stop him. She had been trained as a flight attendant to accede to hijackers' demands.

"'Please sit down and be still, be quiet,'" she pleaded. "Don't draw attention to yourself."

"No," he said. "If they're going to drive this plane into the ground, we've got to do something."

Glick asked his wife for advice. He told her that he and some other men were talking about rushing the hijackers and they were going to take a vote. Then he asked her: "Should we, you know, we're talking about attacking these men, what should I do?"

Lyz hesitated. Then she made a decision.

"Honey, you need to do it." Somehow, his sense of humor was intact enough for him to joke with her.

"OK," he told her. "I have my butter knife from breakfast."

Bingham called his mother over the Airfone to tell her he loved her. He was so rattled, he said, "Hi, Mom, this is Mark Bingham."

During the three minutes that they talked, she said he was distracted twice.

"There was a five-second pause, I heard murmuring, nothing loud," she said. She believes that he and the others were talking about taking back the plane. He barely had the chance to tell her he loved her. Then the phone went dead.

"He doesn't seek out trouble, but he won't run away from it either," she said. "If he sees something wrong, he sets it right."

Beamer told Jefferson he and others were going to "jump on" the hijacker with the bomb, who was guarding the passengers in the rear of the plane. He mentioned Jeremy Glick by name.

"We're going to do something," he told her. "I know I'm not going to get out of this."

At one point, Jefferson heard shouts and commotion. Then Beamer asked her to pray with him. They recited the 23rd Psalm. He made her promise to call his pregnant wife, Lisa, and tell her how much he loved her and his sons, David and Drew. Then he put down the phone.

Jefferson stayed on the line. She heard him say, "Are you ready? OK. Let's roll."

Jefferson and Macklin, Burnett's father-in-law, stayed on the phone as the men sprang into action. They said they heard screams, then silence, then more screams and then nothing. It appears that the plan was for some men to jump the terrorist with the phony bomb in the back of the plane, and for others to storm the cockpit to take control of the plane.

*The Dallas Morning News* reported that at 9:58 EST, eight minutes before the flight crashed, an emergency dispatcher in Westmoreland County, PA, got a cell phone call from a passenger who said he had locked himself into a bathroom on United Airlines Flight 93. He reported that he had heard some kind of explosion. He said the plane was "going down" and he saw white smoke coming from the plane. Then the dispatcher lost contact with him.

Eyewitnesses on the ground said they saw the jet wobble hard left, then right. Perhaps that's indicative of the struggle in the cockpit to take over the plane. Whatever happened, this much is clear. United Flight 93 did not reach the hijackers' target. It was the only hijacked plane that day that was prevented from killing more innocent people on the ground or destroying another American landmark.

The plane was a scant 30 minutes from Washington, DC, when it hit. It came down with such force that it gouged a crater out of what had been a deserted strip mine in rural Somerset County. The point of impact was about 80 miles southeast of Pittsburgh.

Authorities may never know what caused the plane to plummet so quickly, or what accounted for the explosion the unnamed passenger claimed to have heard. Eyewitnesses say they saw an F-16 circling the area. But the accounts they gave convinced some that the plane was not shot down. Investigators did find some lightweight debris—such as insulation and papers—as far as eight miles from the point of impact. However, experts say they could have been carried that far by the wind. In either case, the Pentagon vigorously denies claims that a military plane shot down Flight 93.

Lisa Beamer told NBC's *Dateline* that she was standing behind her couch when she heard newscasters say that the flight that had just gone down was the United flight from Newark to San Francisco. "That's his flight," she said. A friend who was with her tried to reassure her, but she knew.

"No," she said. "I know·that's his flight."

## The Aftermath

WHEN THE STORY began coming together, Americans were awed by the bravery of the men who tried to retake the plane. In October, FBI counter-terrorism director Tim Caruso said there was enough evidence to confirm "that the passengers engaged in a fight for their lives with the four hijackers" and "most likely . . . saved the lives of unknown individuals on the ground." Pennsylvania Senators Rick Santorum and Arlen Specter proposed awarding the men a Presidential Medal of Freedom, the nation's highest civilian honor. Immediately, thousands of Americans jumped on the bandwagon. A Dallas Morning News editorial writer recommended that all of the passengers receive the medal.

The way family members dealt with the deaths is as remarkable as the story of bravery. Weeks after the tragedy, Lisa Beamer boarded the same flight from Newark to California so she could complete her husband's journey and meet with Oracle Company officials about a foundation she has organized to commemorate her husband and provide financial assistance to the victims.

Lyzbeth Glick told NBC's Dateline she wasn't angry or bitter. She believes her husband was fated to be on that plane.

"God or some higher power knew Jeremy somehow had the strength to somehow stop some of the bad that was going on," she said. "I believe that Jeremy was meant for a higher purpose."

# A GOD OF SURPRISES

*"Lord take me where You want me to go; let me meet who You want
me to meet.
Tell me what You want me to say and keep me out of Your Way. "
—Father Mychal Judge*

This was Father Mychal Judge's constant prayer and the words the
Roman Catholic priest lived by. He felt strongly about living a life
surrendered to God no matter what role he played. And he had several.
In one, he was a Franciscan friar, dressed in the long brown robe,
heavy rope belt and sandals of the order founded by St. Francis of
Assisi. Like all Franciscans, he was committed to helping the destitute.
He felt a particularly strong calling to care for the homeless.

In his other role, he was the personable, much-loved chaplain of
the Fire Department of New York City. It was in that role that Judge
was killed on September 11th. He was administering last rites to a
firefighter who had been crushed beneath the body of a woman who
had jumped from an upper-story window of one of the twin towers.
Judge had knelt beside the firefighter and taken off his own helmet to
pray, when he, himself, was felled by debris. Firefighters found him
beneath a smashed fire engine.

They carried Father Judge's body a few blocks to St. Peter's
Church, where they laid him before the altar. Then they carried him to
the two places he loved most. One was Ladder 24, Engine 10, which
was almost directly across the street from his parish, St. Francis of
Assisi. Then they brought him into the church, laid his body in front of
the altar, and covered him with a white cloth and his priest's stole.
They placed his helmet and badge on his chest.

Curiously, Judge's body was the first released from Ground Zero;

his death certificate has No. # 1 on it.

The Rev. Michael Duffy, who delivered the homily as his funeral mass on Sept. 15th, said the timing revealed the hand of God. Judge's "role was to bring the firemen to their death and meet their maker," Duffy told those who had come to pay their respects.

"Two hundred to 300 firemen are still buried there, [so] it would have been physically impossible for him to minister to all of them in this life, but not in the next."

"We're going to have more and more people brought out of that rubble and Mychal Judge is going to greet them on the other side of death," Duffy continued. "He's going to greet them with his big Irish smile. He's going to take them by the hand and say, 'Welcome! Let me take you to our Father.'"

On the morning of September 11th, another priest had spotted a plane flying low over Sixth Avenue and saw the smoke rising from the World Trade Center after it hit. The priest had gone straight to Judge, saying, "I think they're going to need you."

Judge had quickly changed from his friar's habit to his chaplain's uniform and dashed off. After he arrived, he had spent some time with New York Mayor Rudolph Giuliani at the mayor's makeshift command center at the World Trade Center. Before the two men parted, the mayor asked Judge to pray for them.

"I always do," Judge had said with a grin. Word reached Duffy in the afternoon that Judge had been killed. "I felt my whole spirit fall and turn into a pile of rubble at the bottom of my heart," he recalled.

Judge was no stranger to heartbreak himself. As a chaplain, he had witnessed the loss of many of his brother firefighters. But he was philosophical about loss. "My God is a God of surprises," he would always say.

At the funeral, Cardinal Egan stirred the congregation to cheers when he proclaimed that, "New York is going to be rebuilt better and stronger than ever before out of the blood and sweat of our heroes."

The church was packed with brown-robed Franciscan friars, fire department officers in white gloves, and dazed-looking firefighters in bunker pants and dust-coated shirts. Over 2,000 people came to pay tribute to the 68-year-old priest. Mourners included former President Bill Clinton and scores of AIDS sufferers, whose lives Judge had touched.

Judge's grandmother, Vina Drennan, recalled what Judge often said to her after her husband's death seven years earlier. "He used to tell me, All is well,'" she said. "And I didn't believe him."

She paused and softly repeated. "All is well," she said.

Duffy spoke of his conversations with Judge, who he remembered as a happy, fulfilled man.

"He once asked me, 'Do you know what I really need? Absolutely nothing. Why am I so blessed?'"

While the eulogy drew tears, there was also laughter. Duffy recalled Judge's habit of blessing people with his big heavy hands, "even if they didn't ask him to," and his penchant for getting his picture in the newspapers. "He loved to be where the action was," said Duffy. "He loved his fire department and the men in it."

Judge came from humble beginnings. As a boy in Brooklyn, he had earned money shining shoes. His infectious personality and handsome smile soon won him countless friends. Over time, by the sheer force of his personality, he became known to many including New York's elite.

In the month following his funeral, several firefighters took Judge's helmet to Vatican City to present to the Pope. Judge had made several pilgrimages to Rome himself. The Rev. Pat Fitzgerald, who presented the helmet, explained the purpose of doing so.

"It's the primary symbol for the firefighters, but in presenting this helmet to Pope John Paul, it is a deeper symbol," he said. "It is not just Mychal's helmet. It is the helmet of all firefighters of New York." Fitzgerald lived with Judge at the St. Francis monastery. They had entered the seminary together. The date, ironically, was Sept. 11, 1951.

## 19 DECORATIONS IN 21 YEARS

TERENCE HATTON, Captain of Rescue 1, was one of the first firefighters to respond to the call for help on the morning of September 11th. He rushed in to bring people out of the swaying infernos and he was carried out several weeks later, cradled in the arms of his brother firefighters from Rescue 1. His remains were uncovered in the five-story funeral pyre of rubble called "The Pile." He was found alongside another firefighter from his unit, the two of them bringing the number of the dead from Rescue 1 to 11 out of 26 firefighters.

The bodies of the two were draped in the red, white and blue of the American flag. As they were carried out, rescue workers and firefighters slid their dust-encrusted helmets off their heads and saluted their fallen comrades. Thus closed the illustrious career of a sterling firefighter, a man who ran toward danger, using his cool planning and calculated understanding of the risks involved to keep himself and fellow firefighters safe. Never one to be reckless, Hatton emphasized procedure and was a stickler for details. He was also extraordinarily effective. He was decorated 19 times in his 21-year career for his bravery and successful rescues.

Here's just a small sample of what he accomplished. He pulled a woman from a Queens diner leveled by a gas explosion. He was lowered by a rope from a Times Square building roof during a gale force wind, so he could secure a falling billboard endangering passersby below. He was among the leaders of a national urban search and rescue team sent to Oklahoma City after the bombing of the Alfred P. Murray Federal Building. He also rescued people stuck on a disabled elevator on the 78th floor of the World Trade Center.

"It seemed to me that I have given Terry commendations every other week. I don't know if there are any more commendations," said New York Mayor Rudolph Giuliani.

But Hatton's intelligence and strategic thinking were no match for the millions of tons of metal and concrete that would rain down on him on September 11th.

As decorated as he was, the then 41-year-old had a life outside the fire station. He was a confirmed bachelor until just five years before 9/11 when he fell hard for Beth Petrone, the longtime assistant of the mayor of New York.

"Theirs was a love story that movies are made of, a love story that everyone wished they had," said Richard Sheirer, director of the city's Office of Emergency Management. Sheirer had played Cupid for the pair.

From the time they met, the two were inseparable and crazy in love. In 1998, Mayor Giuliani officiated at their one-of-a-kind wedding, which was held at Gracie Mansion.

"Terry was the kind of guy I want my son to be like," said the mayor. "It was one of the most beautiful weddings I did. She was madly in love with him from the first moment she saw him, and he with her."

The news that his remains had been found took their toll on Petrone Hatton, who managed to focus on the positive memories and their time together. She told friends and family that she was proud to have known and loved him for five years. She knew what she had was special and worth honoring, and she was lucky to have experienced it all.

And she knew something else. Shortly after September 11th, she learned that her husband had left her with a lasting piece of himself—a child.

"There is a miracle," Giuliani recalls her saying. "The doctor found a heartbeat. I'm pregnant."

Although their time together has ended, the couple's love continues. As does Hatton's legacy—in the hearts of firefighters, the people he saved, his wife and his child.

## NOT YOUR TYPICAL NEW YORK COP

CAPTAIN JOHN PERRY did not fit the profile of a New York City police officer. For one thing, he was a lawyer, and a very articulate one at that. He spoke five languages. He had once worked in the advocate's office for the New York Police Department, where he prosecuted "bad cops." He was also an actor. He served in the National Guard.

"He was a Renaissance man who always had a sparkle in his eye and a winning smile," said friend and former head of the NY Civil Liberties Union Norman Siegel.

September 11th was to be his last day on the beat. The 38-year-old cop had taken the day off from the 40th precinct in the Bronx to turn in his retirement papers. He planned to start his own law practice.

Instead, like so many other police officers that day, he bolted out of police headquarters when he heard that a plane had smashed into one of the Twin Towers. He wanted to help. It would be his last act.

Perry met up with Police Capt. Timothy Pearson and his crew of police officers on his way to the disaster site. They headed into the north tower through the concourse below the plaza. Firefighters in front of Pearson and Perry asked them to take an unconscious woman out of the building. He grabbed her under one arm, Perry under the other.

"Then all of a sudden we heard this rumbling. The lights flickered, then went completely black." The south tower had begun to collapse; Pearson, dazed and barely able to breathe, saw a small light in the distance. He heard someone yell, "Over here, this way." He followed the light, and 10 minutes later, was safely outside. The concourse was now ablaze from leaking jet fuel pouring from the elevator shafts.

The north tower fell with incredible force just moments later, burying Capt. John Perry. The light had saved Timothy Pearson.

"John was only an arm's length away from me when everything came down on us," said Pearson. "I guess he never saw the light."

# A ROOKIE WITH A HERO'S HEART

WATCHING EACH OTHER'S BACK, making sure that you don't leave anybody behind—that is what is expected of police officers. But the bond goes much deeper that, as we saw on September 11th. So many risked their lives for their colleagues without a second's thought. Port Authority Police Officer Dominick Pezzulo was one of them. He was on the force less than a year, which makes his selfless act of heroism even more poignant.

Pezzulo was assigned to the Port Authority Bus Terminal when the first plane hit. He and his colleagues commandeered a city bus and had the driver race to the scene so they could help with the rescue efforts. Pezzulo saved the lives of two city cops when he rushed into one of the towers. When the towers collapsed, he found himself buried under the choking debris with another officer not far from him. Pezzulo managed to free himself, but he couldn't leave his fellow officer behind.

Going back for his fellow officer cost him his life.

"Dominick dug himself out of the rubble to safety," the Rev. Donald Dwyer said at the funeral mass for the 36-year-old Port Authority police officer. "But when he realized that a fellow officer was still covered in rubble, still inside, he returned through the rubble, through the same tunnel that he helped dig, to save a comrade, to save a brother. He died trying to save the life of a fellow police officer."

The wife and two children of the Port Authority police officer can take solace in knowing he died a hero.

"He gave his heart and life to the job," said Ralph Balsamo, of the Balsamo Funeral Home in the Bronx. "He is a fallen hero."

# THE REACH OF A FATHER'S LOVE

SISTERS TIFFANY and Yolanda Smith were the twin apples of their father's eye. His name was Leon Smith, and he had been a firefighter with Ladder 118/Engine 205 for 19 years. He was among the more than 300 firefighters who died at the Twin Towers.

On the morning of September 11th, Smith was at the Brooklyn Heights Firehouse with his colleagues when they heard the fire bell. "Express" Smith, as he was known for his speed and adeptness, drove the rig across the Brooklyn Bridge to lower Manhattan. They parked their rig and vanished somewhere inside the thick clouds of black smoke and grit that engulfed the site. None of the six were seen again.

The Ladder 118 truck was recovered days later. Its windows were broken and its cab was filled with twisted steel. It has since been restored, but the men who rode in it will never do so again.

When his daughters learned what happened to their father, they were beside themselves with grief. But they knew all too well the danger their dad faced daily. The twins knew that their father would have wanted to die doing what he loved best.

One of Leon's friends, Vernon Cherry, left a wife of 31 years. For Joanne Cherry there's a comfort knowing that the men died in the line of duty.

"Maybe this was the way Vernon wanted to leave the world," she said. "I don't wish the truck turned around. I know in my heart he would have wanted to go full blast in there. He would have never turned back. His job was saving people. He loved this job."

The same could be said about Leon Smith.

"He loved it there," said Tiffany. "I used to ask him, Are you sure this is what you want to do? You're not scared?' And he would always say he loved it, he would die for it. That's what he did."

Dealing with their grief was one thing. But there were practical concerns as well. Who would provide financial support? Smith's deepest desire was to see his daughters graduate from college.

"All Leon talked about was his girls, and how he wanted them to go to college, how he was hoping they would get basketball scholarships," said fellow firefighter Richie Murray.

The girls were enrolled as freshmen at Johnson C. Smith University in North Carolina. But who would pay the tuition now?

Then something wonderful happened. A month after they lost their father, the girls learned that they were being awarded full scholarships. They knew their dad was behind it.

"He must still be looking out for all of us from above," said Murray. The girls enjoyed the added thrill of receiving the scholarships from the President and First Lady.

"Even though he can't be here physically, he is still here spiritually," said Tiffany. "Even though this was a disaster, good things happened because of him."

## NEW TO AMERICA, BUT NOT TO BRAVERY

WHEN DISASTER STRIKES, the natural impulse is to flee. But Zhe Zeng didn't.

Zeng, a Chinese American, had just gotten off the subway at the Brooklyn Bridge stop when the first plane struck. He was out of harm's way. The then 29-year-old was on his way to his job as a project manager at the Bank of New York's Barclay Street office. When Zeng saw what happened, he ran to work, but stayed only long enough to pick up supplies and medical equipment. He was an emergency medical technician and knew he could help.

Then he raced back out with his supplies, running through the rain of debris, thick soot and ash. "It didn't surprise anybody who knew him," said Peggy Farrell, his supervisor. "He was a completely selfless person-someone who would automatically volunteer his assistance."

A local news video showed him, still in his business suit, giving medical assistance to someone lying on the ground. He was focused on helping and seemed oblivious to the danger he had put himself in.

That was the last time anyone saw him.

"It was a truly heroic display," said Farrell.

# HE WAS CHANTYL'S HERO FIRST

CHANTYL PETERSON OWED her life to New York City firefighter Terrence Farrell. But this was an unusual kind of rescue. She wasn't in a burning building, or trapped with no means of escape. In fact, the then 13-year-old Las Vegas girl would not meet him until a year after he had saved her life. Farrell gave Peterson something she couldn't get from anyone else—his perfectly matched bone marrow.

At age 4, Chantyl had been diagnosed with T-cell lymphoma. She was so ill, she was hardly able to do more than lie in bed. She was too frail to play. Her only hope for survival was a marrow transplant. Thanks to a nationwide database that matches people's bone marrow with the terminally ill, she was matched with Terrence Farrell. Farrell's bone marrow had been entered into the database in 1989, when he was a probationary firefighter. That's standard procedure for everyone who enters the Fire Academy. The bone-marrow sampling is then registered in the database.

In 1993, when Farrell found out he could save a little girl's life, he did not hesitate to say Yes. He knew the procedure would be painful, but that didn't stop him.

The match worked. Peterson was cured.

The Queens, NY, man, a firefighter with Rescue Co. 4, finally met Chantyl a year later. They had lunch in—of all places—a restaurant on the 87th floor of the World Trade Center. The firefighter and the little girl became fast friends. They planned to meet every five years, forever.

But Farrell never made it again to his reunion with the young recipient of his marrow. The strapping firefighter was one of the 343 members of the Fire Department of New York who gave their lives to save others on September 11th.

Chantyl did not take the news well. Farrell had been her hero.

"The man moved mountains for us," said Chantyl's mother Sheri. She brought her daughter to New York for Farrell's funeral more than a month later. "I had to bring Chantyl so she could say goodbye. She was in a pretty deep state of denial that Terry could be gone. Up until the moment we got the call that they found him, every time the phone rang, I was expecting to hear his voice saying that he was OK."

Chantyl Peterson lost her hero that day. Her room was plastered with photographs of the man to whom she owed her life. She will never forget him, she said.

"I remember every little detail about Terry. He'd always give me hugs and give me speeches about his job. I felt so angry and sad at the same time when this happened. I wish I could give him a hug. He gave me so many hugs."

Chantyl's mother is struck by the fact that after 9/11 everyone would also know the measure of the man who gave her back her daughter.

"He was always Chantyl's handsome hero," she said. "Now he's America's hero, too."

# NO STRANGER TO DANGER

PORT AUTHORITY POLICE Officer George Howard was off-duty September 11th. He had planned to enjoy it. He was sitting in front of his computer at home in Hicksville, NY, when he heard that the World Trade Center had been hit by a plane. He didn't think twice. It didn't matter that it was his day off. Instinct took over. He left his home, sped to his post at Kennedy Airport and hopped a rescue truck headed for lower Manhattan. He made it to the Twin Towers moments before the second tower collapsed.

A giant slab of metal felled him. His body was found in front of the place where the towers once stood.

"He didn't have to go, but he did anyway," said the Rev. James Devine, a Port Authority chaplain. "George gave his life saving others, not only on September 11th. He spent a lifetime saving others."

Days after the disaster, Arlene Howard presented her son's badge to President Bush as he met with relatives of missing cops and firefighters.

The then 44-year-old Howard was no stranger to danger. The 16-year veteran was one of the original founding members of the Port Authority's elite emergency services. Howard took his work very seriously, making it more than full time. When he wasn't working as a police officer at John F. Kennedy Airport, he was volunteering as a firefighter in his spare time. He was so dedicated to public service that he spent hours training other police and fire departments in safety and rescue work. Somehow he also found time to coach soccer and lacrosse for his son's teams.

Howard was modest about his accomplishments. He considered heroics part of the job. He shrugged off compliments. This was true, even when the city applauded him for this courage when terrorists bombed the World Trade Center in 1993. Howard led 62 panicked schoolchildren through the darkness, as they groped their way to safety. The children were stuck in an elevator and probably near hysteria until Howard showed up to rescue them. To him, it was no big deal.

He told the press at the time, "Everybody just did their job. That's what they pay us for."

People who knew Howard well weren't surprised to learn that he raced to the scene on his day off. "He gave, and he gave without hesitation," said his friend Kevin Hasset, a Port Authority police lieutenant. "He was an individual ready to face danger."

"He died saving people's lives," said Arlene Howard. "There's nothing greater than that." His brother, Patrick, a New York Police Department sergeant, spoke at the funeral and told his brother, posthumously, "I am sorry I couldn't be there to save you."

But amidst the sorrow, there was remembrance of the spirit that drove Howard throughout his life.

"When it's my time and I find the gates of heaven closed, I will yell through the gates for George," said Hasset. "If anyone knows how to get through that gate, it's George."

# AN 'IN-CHARGE' KIND OF GUY

THOMAS E. GORMAN, an 18-year veteran of the Port Authority police, was on desk duty in the Port Authority's World Trade Center office on September 11th. The then-41-year-old Middlesex, NJ, father of three was called to action shortly after the first plane struck.

"As far as we know, he was called and assigned to the lobby at Tower One," said Pat Reiner, a close friend of Gorman and his family. "After that, the video showed him with another officer going into the ER unit of the Port Authority, which put him in the tower just five minutes before the building collapsed."

Hours after the attacks, Reiner and Diane Concannon, another close friend of the Gormans, had held out hope that he had survived. They helped his wife, Barbara call all the area hospitals, to see whether they could locate him. Their hope was buoyed by a call from a St. Claire Hospital employee early that evening. The employee, who identified herself as a nurse, gave them erroneous information that he had been treated and released, and would return home by police escort.

They were overjoyed. They even organized an impromptu coming home party for him. They fully expected to see him again.

"If anyone could survive that, it would have been him. He was just that kind of guy," said Reiner, her voice filled with admiration. "I really expected him to walk out of the rubble with 20 people behind him."

But Gorman never returned. Hospital staff said later that there was no record that he'd been treated there. His wife held a service for him that October, even though he was still listed among the missing.

All in all, 74 Port Authority police and civilians were lost in the September 11th attacks on the World Trade Center. That's more than five times the number killed during the previous 73 years. Among the dead were Capt. Kathy Mazza of Farmingdale, NY, the first female Port Authority officer killed in the line of duty.

About 2,000 administrative staff of the Port Authority of New York and New Jersey worked in offices there. When the buildings collapsed, the organization lost its headquarters and its executive director, Neil Levin. Understandably, the organization took the attack personally. As Lt. Susan Durett, a supervisor, remarked, "This was our house."

Until the September 11th attacks, the Port Authority police didn't attract much notice. Unlike the New York Police Department, they have not inspired any police shows. But they do important—if not exactly glamorous—work. Port Authority police protect millions of people who use the city's transportation facilities, including the airports, railways, bus terminals, PATH trains and the bridges of New York and New Jersey.

When the first plane hit the north tower on September 11th, Port Authority police throughout the city sprang into action. They evacuated approximately 2,000 passengers from a PATH train under the World Trade Center complex. Inspector Timothy Norris, who arrived on the scene eight minutes after the first plane hit, rushed to the command center at One World Trade Center, where he helped terrified tenants evacuate.

"I remember this lady covered in dust, holding my arm," he said. "She looked at my name tag and kept saying, 'T. Norris, T. Norris, just lead me to safety.'"

Which he did. He later saw an arm protruding out of the rubble. He and another man helped pull the survivor out, disregarding the danger to themselves.

Such self-sacrifice was the order of the day. Gorman, like many of the fallen policemen in the Trade Center tragedy, was committed to doing for others.

"When my house flooded during Hurricane Floyd, he had just come off a 17-hour shift," Reiner recalled. "He came to my house to help me with the mess, and then had my whole family over for a meatloaf dinner at his house."

"He was an in-charge type of guy," said Concannon. "If there was a situation that needed it, he did what had to get done. We're all very proud of him. I have no doubt that he made sure he could get as many people out of there as possible. He gave up his life doing that. He's a hero to us."

# WESTFIELD AMERICA'S HEROIC VP

IT IS ANYONE'S GUESS how many people could have gotten out of the Twin Towers safely but gave their lives to save others. Bruce Eagleson was one of them.

A vice president of Westfield America, which had its offices in the south tower, Eagleson was in charge of 11 employees. The Connecticut man took his responsibility very seriously. When the plane struck the tower, his employees were his first concern. He focused on making sure all of them escaped. Witnesses said he kept going back to the building, to the other offices, to make sure that as many people as he could find were evacuated. He was last seen returning to his office to get two-way radios. He thought it would help if they could communicate with each other as they descended the stairwells.

"We are so overwhelmed by the heroism of those many people on September 11th," said the Rev. John Ashe of St. John's during his eulogy at Eagleson's memorial service. "It was Bruce who made sure all who worked for him got out of that building."

Eagleson was a big-hearted man with genuine concern for others, concern that he exhibited at a young age. During his teen years, a time when so many kids are fixated on their own popularity, Eagleson gave swimming lessons to handicapped children. He even organized a fundraiser for the group that was offering the lessons. Eagleson managed to attract three well-known sports figures to draw people to the fundraiser.

"That was the Bruce that I remember," said his brother William. "He was determined to do the best all the time."

If the measure of a life is how much one is missed, Eagleson—like so many of the husbands, sons and fathers that day—had a life of tremendous magnitude.

"The more it hurts, the more I know he was such a great dad," said his youngest son Brett.

## "WHAT WOULD YOU EXPECT ME TO DO?"

THE TALMUD SAYS that if you save one life you have saved the world. Well, Alayne Gentul, a Mountainside, NJ mother of two, must have saved the world 40 times over. The chairman of Fiduciary Trust Co. credits his former human resources director with saving at least that many lives on the morning of September 11th.

Gentul, who would have turned 45 on Oct. 4, 2001, was the kind of person people turned to for direction. And that morning, the 700 employees who worked with her in the 90th through 97th floors in the south tower of the World Trade Center looked to her again. At that point, confusion reigned. American Flight 11, a Boeing 767, had slammed into the north tower next door. Steven Tall, chief technology officer for the company, had seen the fire as he drove into work from his New Jersey home, and called to alert the company's disaster recovery personnel.

Fiduciary Trust employees didn't know what to do. Someone who had access to the public address system in the south tower ordered people to go back to their offices. "This building is safe," he had said. Another employee thought it best if everyone waited for the fire marshals.

But not Alayne.

Nora Haldon remembered her standing at the door leading to the 90th floor. "What do you want us to do?" Haldon had asked her.

"Nora, everyone should go downstairs in an orderly way. Go now." Gentul held the door open as the other employees filed through it. Haldon remembered how calm she was.

Then Gentul went upstairs. She knew that the technical-support employees on the 97th floor were busy backing up all electronic records of client accounts, trades and money transfers. The call from Tall prompted them to execute the company's comprehensive disaster recovery plan so Fiduciary wouldn't lose critical data.

People who knew Alayne well weren't surprised that she went upstairs to evacuate the others.

"It was her nature to always put other people first, and I'm not just referring to Tuesday, but every day," said her friend, Allison Katz, a manager in her department.

Gentul called her husband, Jack, from the 97th floor. She told him that she found eight employees huddled there, holding wet clothes over their mouths. Smoke was pouring through the vents. They didn't know what was happening. Had the fire spread from the other tower? Were they better off staying or leaving?

"I'm not sure we can get out," she told her husband.

Jack, dean of students at the New Jersey Institute of Technology, stayed on the phone with his wife and called out for his colleagues to help. Someone called the 911 operator to let them know Gentul and others were trapped on the 97th floor. The 911 operator had advised them to stay put. Someone else called the security officer at the south tower to find out whether they'd advise Gentul and the others to stay put or try to evacuate. The south tower security guard recommended that they try to leave the building. Another gave advice on how to trip the sprinkler system, but the advice didn't work. The group decided to try to evacuate. They were running out of time.

Alayne told her husband she was scared. She let him know how much she loved him and asked him to tell the same to her two sons, Alex and Robbie, 12 and 8 years old, respectively. They were the lights of her life. She would leave home at 6:30 every morning so she could return in time to put dinner on the table for her family at a reasonable hour. She "did for them" on the weekends, biking with them, playing their favorite games.

While they were on the phone, Jack Gentul said he heard a large explosion. He later assumed he had heard American Airlines Flight 175, a Boeing 757, slam into the south tower below the floors where Fiduciary Trust Co. had its offices. He knew he had to let her go. After they declared their love for each other, over and over again, he did.

He would later tell *The Newark Star Ledger* that it was the hardest thing he ever had to do in his life.

He paced his office, praying urgently that his wife and her colleagues would make it out.

Nora Haldon, who was about a block away from the south tower when the second plane hit, looked back when she heard the explosion.

"I knew Alayne would still be in there," said Haldon. "As long as there were still people upstairs, she wouldn't have come out. That was just Alayne." She knew Alayne would never make it out then.

So did Jack Gentul. As he stood there praying, he felt Alayne pass through him.

"I knew she was gone," he said.

So after what must have been a horrible death, this very special woman— who'd taught Sunday school kindergarten for nine years at Community Church in Mountain Lakes, NJ—momentarily merged her soul with that of the man she loved. It was her way of saying goodbye.

Because of her, at least 40 other families of Fiduciary Trust Co. would not suffer the pain of loss that her family does.

Jack Gentul took some consolation from the fact that his wife, a board trustee at her church, died helping others. But there were moments when he naturally felt anger over his loss. One time, he said, he cried out in despair, "Why did you do it?"

Miraculously, she answered him in a voice he heard within himself.

"What would you expect me to do?" she had replied.

Of course, he already knew the answer.

# THE END OF AN ERA

THE DEATH OF First Deputy Commissioner William M. Feehan—and with it, his experience and expertise—marks the end of an era in the New York City Fire Department.

So read the final sentence of the department's memorial to one of its best-loved members. Bill Feehan, a veteran firefighter who joined the department in 1959, held every title within the department during his 42 years there. He progressed from a "proby" or probationary firefighter, to full-time firefighter, to lieutenant, to chief, to deputy fire commissioner and finally, acting fire commissioner.

The 71-year-old Feehan stayed on the job long after he could have retired because he loved it and long after most men would have been pushed out because he was loved. His firefighters loved him as much as his family members did. He loved them in return. His men felt his love and gravitated toward him, said one official.

"They all needed Bill Feehan to tell them what to do." Those who knew him said he was the "heart and soul" of the department and "the guy who knew everything." The Rev. Brian Barr, who delivered his eulogy, said Feehan was "the type of guy who made everyone feel special. What made him such a great father also made him a great fire chief."

"Bill Feehan was not just one of the great leaders of the fire department," said Fire Commissioner Thomas Von Essen, who also spoke at Feehan's funeral. "He was a friend."

Feehan was the son of a fireman and had a son in the department. He insisted on being called "chief" even after serving as acting FDNY commissioner in the last months of the Dinkins' administration. Former Mayor David Dinkins' successors never asked Feehan to step aside for new appointees, and City Council Speaker Peter Vallone explained why at his funeral.

"He was the power behind the throne," said Vallone. "They all needed Bill Feehan to tell them what to do, to be the rock, the strong hands."

Former department spokesman Michael Regan said that the veteran chief, who reputedly knew the location of every hydrant in the city, "was not going to retire because the fire department was his lifeblood."

His son, William, spoke of his father's special relationship with each of his children, though he "loved being a firefighter more than anything. There was no place on Earth that my father would rather be than at a fire scene," he said. "He was loved by so many people; he loved so many people. He lived every second of his life without regret."

While the church was packed, many of the men who would have come under any other circumstances to pay their respects to the beloved Feehan skipped the memorials so they could continue with the macabre but necessary task of looking for remains. "Bill wouldn't have wanted it any other way," said one of the grim-faced mourners who filed past his coffin.

As Feehan's casket was draped with the cream-colored flag of the New York Fire Department, many paid the homage he so deeply deserved. Feehan had entered public service very early. He was a well-decorated war veteran who served the army in Korea before he became a firefighter.

# RESCUE, SEARCH, RECOVERY

## A VOICE IN THE DARK

It was a booming voice, rich, resonant, deep in its timber. A voice that compelled one to pay attention. A voice that was easy to follow. Its tone: reassuring, yet commanding. A voice to be listened to. And by listening to it, at least eight people were led out of harm's way.

Wayne Sinclair was one of them. The then-54-year-old computer programmer was in his office in the Pentagon when the hijacked plane hit the building. The blast leveled his office and knocked him to the ground. Bloodied, disoriented and covered in soot, Sinclair crawled around on the floor, desperate for a way out. Thick, black smoke and choking heat engulfed him, throwing him into a panic. He was afraid he might not make it out alive. But then he heard it. A voice, clear and deep, pierced the darkness surrounding him.

"Head toward my voice," it said. He did, as did seven of his colleagues. As he crawled forward, unsure of where he was heading, he allowed himself to trust that voice. There was hope in that voice. "There's an opening out here."

Within minutes, Sinclair was through the blackness and the heat. He gasped sporadically to take in as much fresh air as his lungs would allow. His body was burning and his skin was charred black. The smoke stung and clouded his eyes and ash obstructed his vision, making it impossible to open them. He tried to get a glance of the man whose voice had led him to safety, but his eyes would not allow him. By the time he could open his eyes enough to take in the scene around him, the man with the commanding voice had vanished.

Sinclair was taken to the hospital. He suffered from second- and third- degree burns on his arms and legs, and had more minor injuries. He spent over three weeks in the hospital undergoing treatment and wondering about the man whose voice had saved his life.

The voice that Sinclair was so desperately seeking belonged to Isaac Hoopii, an officer with the police bomb detection canine unit at the Pentagon. In addition to his full-time job, Hoopii was also a lead singer and guitar player for a Hawaiian band, Aloha Boys, which played the Washington, DC, circuit. But the burly Hawaiian's deeply resonant voice served a much greater purpose that day, one that makes his singing career pale in comparison.

The day the plane struck the Pentagon, Hoopii was at the veterinarian's office with his canine partner, Vito. Their visit was cut short by a radio alert he received on his two-way radio, reporting trouble at the Pentagon. He hit the lights and siren on his cruiser and sped to the scene, blowing his transmission in his frenetic haste to get there. He joined other Pentagon police officers and rescue workers who were already pulling people out of the burning building and struggling to keep their own composure.

"Your adrenaline is pumping so fast because you just want to get in there and help people," said the 6' 2", 260-lb. father of three. In the course of his rescue work, he carried a woman out who couldn't walk, and when he lifted her in his arms, "the flesh just fell off."

In the frenzy that was the first few hours of that day, Hoopii carried and led people out of the inferno. But after firefighters held him back from rushing into the black billowing smoke on the first floor, he knew he needed to find another way to rescue those screaming "voices in the dark" he heard, begging for help. He put his booming baritone to good use, calming the frightened and telling them to follow his voice.

Like many of the rescue heroes that day, Hoopii said he felt empty afterward. That's typical of rescuers, and it stems from the uncertainty they feel. Were lives actually saved? Could they have done more? Not knowing the answers can haunt them.

When Hoopii discovered that there was a survivor, someone looking for a man with a distinctive larger-than-life voice, the emptiness lifted. The two men met a month after the incident. Sinclair hugged his 260-pound guardian angel in a long, tight embrace. Tears welled up in their eyes as the two strangers held each other.

Up until September 11th, Isaac would have been delighted to be known for his distinctive singing voice. Being able to use his voice to lead people to safety has given it a much richer meaning. Now, he knows it was meant for a much higher purpose.

## IN SAVING ANOTHER, THEY SAVED THEMSELVES

WHEN HE FIRST HEARD the explosion, John Jonas, then Fire Captain of Ladder Company 6, assumed that a truck had plunged off the Manhattan Bridge into the murky depths of the East River. But firefighter Matt Komorowski, who was standing outside, saw the plane as it slipped between the Twin Towers with a colossal explosion. Their firehouse is on Canal Street in Chinatown, just blocks from where the Twin Towers once stood. So they made it to the scene in minutes, along with firefighters Bill Butler, Tommy Falco, Mike Meldrum and Sal D'Agostino.

As they got off the truck, particles of metal, debris and dust rained down on them. Butler remembers computers from the upper-floor offices hitting the ground right near the truck. It made it hard for them to get the gear off the truck, but they managed, running with it through the debris into the lobby of One World Trade Center. They got inside just minutes before the second plane struck Two World Trade Center, next door.

Once inside, they each hoisted 100 pounds of gear on their backs and began the ascent up the stairwells. They had to move single-file because the stairwells were so narrow; they permitted only two people abreast. Workers who were evacuating the building were coming down the stairwell to get out. Only one stairwell went straight through to the lobby.

It was tough going. At each 10-story interval, they paused to rest and regain strength. When they reached the 27th floor, they felt the building shudder violently as its twin suddenly collapsed. A fire captain from another company was able to confirm that the south tower had collapsed.

"OK, if that building can go, this building can go," Jonas yelled to his crew as he directed them back down the stairs. Around the 12th floor, they met up with Battalion Chief Richie Piciotto, who was handing off disabled and fatigued building employees to firefighters who could help them evacuate. That's how Josephine Harris, a then-59-year old grandmother who worked for the Port Authority, came under the care of Ladder Company 6. She had walked down from the 73rd floor and she was exhausted.

Jonas told Bill Butler, Ladder 6's strongest man, to throw his arm around her and help her down. She was having a lot of difficulty walking, so she slowed them down considerably.

"C'mon, c'mon! We've got to keep moving," Jonas thought nervously to himself, conscious of the clock ticking in his head. He was well aware that their tower could go, too, and he didn't know how much time they might have left. They stepped aside to let other firefighters pass them. Everyone was racing to get out.

"You've got to pick up the pace here," Butler reminded Harris as he shifted his weight to help her. "Your grandchildren and your kids want to see you at home." Tom Falco stationed himself on the other side of Josephine, so he could help Butler lift her. When she reached the fourth floor, she couldn't go any farther.

"That's it," she said. "I can't go anymore."

Capt. Jonas dashed out of the stairwell, into some fourth-floor offices to look for a chair or other piece of furniture they could carry Harris on. He returned empty-handed.

Suddenly, the entire tower began to collapse. There was thunderous noise as the 110-story steel structure fell down around them, trapping them in the section of stairwell between the fourth and second floors. A blast of wind rushed up the passageway, knocking everyone down. Komorowski, who had been the last in line, was propelled forward through the air, landing two stories below the rest.

He remembers "unbelievable noise. Everything flying around. Tremendous dust clouds. I'm thinking, 'I can't believe this is how it ends for me.'"

All the men were sure they were going to die. They were just waiting for the rest of it to hit.

Miraculously, it didn't. When the rumbling and the movement stopped, they were covered with layer upon layer of pulverized concrete and other debris. The dust was so thick that it made them gag. They could hear each other coughing. The men called to each other by name. Sure enough, they were all still alive, all conscious—including Josephine. She had landed by Bill Butler's feet and was covered with sheetrock and dust. They helped to clean the debris off her, and then put a body harness on her, because they fully intended to carry her out of the building now that the rumbling had stopped.

But they couldn't find a way out.

Komorowski had landed at the bottom of what was left of the stairwell. Beneath him, was only rubble, cement and sheetrock. There was no longer a passage to the first floor landing. They were going to need to think their way out of this. It looked likely that they were going to need to be rescued themselves. So they used the means at their disposal—their radios, a cell phone, a bullhorn—to help rescuers find them. The piles of rubble and the fires surrounding the building impeded their rescue for several hours.

Then the dust cleared. The men were able to find an opening where they could climb out. They knew they'd need help with Josephine, so they signaled to rescuers. Then, continuing to put Josephine Harris' safety first, they waited with her until the rescuers were able to come for her.

It was only later that the men realized the enormity of what had happened. The entire building—with the exception of that two-story stretch of stairwell where they found themselves when the tower crumbled—had collapsed. Their fire engine was flattened under tons of debris. But they were still alive.

And that's when the thought occurred to them. If they had actually been going just a little bit faster, they would not have been in one of the few pockets of the skyscraper that did not collapse. Josephine Harris, who was to turn 60 that same week, had saved their lives.

"We all thought she was going too slow, but she had the perfect pace," said Komorowski. To thank her, Ladder Company 6 gave Harris one of the ladder company's jackets. They had the words "Josephine, Our Guardian Angel" embroidered on it.

Call it luck, call it fate, call it God, call it whatever you want. Matt Komorowski, Mike Meldrum, Bill Butler, Tom Falco, Sal D'Agostino and Capt. John Jonas lived because they were less concerned about their safety than Josephine's. As Capt. Jonas said later: "God gave us courage and strength to save her, and unknowingly, we saved ourselves."

## ROSELLE KNEW JUST WHAT TO DO

ROSELLE WOULDN'T LEAVE Michael Hingson behind. There was just no way. Despite the danger to herself, she was dogged in her determination to make sure that Hingson wasn't among the casualties in the north tower. Except for two other employees, Hingson was virtually alone. Nearly everyone else in his 78th story office was in the process of evacuating the building, which had been set afire by the crash of American Airlines Flight 11. But the then-51 -year-old New Jersey man couldn't get out by himself. He was blind.

The sound and feel of the room engulfed him and sent a chill through his body. He was filled with a foreboding that something horrendous had just happened. An earthquake veteran from California, Hingson noticed the similarity between the rocking motion of the skyscraper and the natural disasters through which he had lived.

With no eyesight to guide him, Hingson had to rely on his instincts and courage. And Roselle. He reached down for the leathery harness, unsure of what he would find. What he felt was the soft furry head of his devoted companion, Roselle, a yellow Labrador retriever service dog.

"She had already jumped up from the floor," Hingson remembered. "Usually she doesn't even stir when the wind shakes the tower."

Roselle was ready to go to work. Hingson issued orders to his new guide dog that had only been with him for nine months. The office was getting hotter by the minute, as she guided him through the disheveled rooms, with toppled filing cabinets, overturned furniture and swirls of paper scattered everywhere. But Hingson couldn't see any of that. He had to rely on Roselle to safely guide him to the stairwell.

As they entered the staircase, they were nearly overcome by the nauseating stench of jet fuel fumes. The heat was oppressive in the cramped stairway, and the dour stink of jet fuel made it hard to breathe.

"The crowds weren't huge at first," Hingson said. "But as we started making our way down, they got bigger."

As they slowly descended, Roselle carefully picked out the steps in front of her. Her panting grew stronger and more labored but she pushed on. At about the 50th floor, Hingson became aware of a small commotion of people rushing past him. He was alarmed at first. They were going the wrong way—up the stairs. Then he realized who they were.

"I heard the applause and was told they were firefighters," he recalled. "I clapped a few on the back, but I was scared for where they were going."

Given the unbearable heat on the 50th floor, he worried what it might be like closer to the top floors where those brave men were headed. Later reports would confirm that temperatures in the north tower rose to a scorching 1,000 degrees and kept climbing.

Every time the doors opened at one of the floors they were passing, a new burst of heat would pass through the crowd, as people descended the stairwell. Hingson, struggling to keep his footing and apace with everyone else, grew more and more concerned about his canine friend. "A lot of pipes had broken and there were puddles on the floor," he said. "Roselle was stopping to drink some of the water, so I knew she was very thirsty."

And indeed she was. Working her way down the stairs in a full coat of fur in the sweltering temperatures must have nearly dehydrated her. Although those around them remained calm, the pace quickened appreciably. Hingson grew fearful that they wouldn't make it.

But despite the anxious, pushing crowds of people around her, the unbearable heat and the terrifying screeching of steel melting all around her, the dog kept going, sure-footed and focused. The fear in the stairwell was palpable, making the final minutes before they reached the lobby particularly harrowing. It took them 50 minutes to get down the stairs and another 10 to get out onto the street.

"I heard the second tower collapsing," Hingson said. "It sounded like a metal and concrete waterfall. We started running for the subway."

There were piercing shrieks of terror then. But Roselle never panicked. She remained focused on her task of getting him to safety. To aid her, Hingson kept the commands simple—left, right—as a police officer steered them into the subway, away from the smoldering buildings.

When they emerged from underground, Hingson learned that the north tower had collapsed and the south tower was smoldering near the top.

A shudder went through him. "It was unbelievable. I felt lucky to be out of there. But I wondered about the firefighters," he said, recalling the sense of dread he felt as the strong elbows and shoulders of those fearless men brushed past him.

Less than 20 minutes later, the south tower gave a final shrug and caved in. A vast, fast-moving gray cloud of ash, glass and debris rolled violently toward Hingson and Roselle, who were still close enough to get caught in the debris. Hingson felt the rush of air that almost knocked them over.

"The air was filled with crud," he said. "A woman nearby couldn't see because she had stuff in her eyes, so Roselle and I helped her."

As the wave of soot from the 110-story building settled in the air, Roselle's shiny yellow coat took on the tinge of dull grayness.

Roselle probably didn't understand what happened that day. But it was more than good training that compelled her to save her master's life. It was her pure animal heart, her canine loyalty that saved them both. Lassie couldn't have done any better.

## 500 PRESENT AND ACCOUNTED FOR

FOURTEEN STORIES, 500 teenagers. That's what Ada Rosairo Dolch was thinking as she made some quick calculations. How do you get 500 teenagers, most of whom have just witnessed the most traumatic event of their lives, out of the building quickly, across a busy highway and to the safety of a park over half a mile away? But that was the task at hand for this principal of the High School for Leadership and Public Service.

"We're going to evacuate," Dolch called into her two-way radio to the school's staff and faculty. The school is right next door to the American Stock Exchange. Everything happened so quickly that day that Dolch had to make life-and-death decisions on the spot. The second plane had just struck the south tower, Two World Trade Center.

As Dolch made the decision to evacuate the students, faculty and staff, so did principals at all the other schools in the financial district. All together, at roughly the same time, they moved over 9,000 kindergarten to high school students out of the buildings and onto the streets of lower Manhattan. The move had to be orderly and calm. And she had to delegate. Luckily, she had dedicated faculty and staff, and students she could count on.

"I thanked every teacher as they came down," she said. "And I said, 'Your job is to stay with your kids as best you can and just walk them into the park, and as deep into the park as you can. You want to be away from the tall buildings.' Some of the kids were crying. Some of the kids were shaking."

Of course they were traumatized. Many of them had seen what had happened. The large, 14-story reconverted building had three huge windows per classroom, all looking out onto the World Trade Center. Most of the teenagers had their eyes glued to the windows and had witnessed not only the crashes, but also the deaths of those people falling or jumping from the buildings. The impact of such large-scale destruction was devastating.

"One of my students came down. He couldn't talk. But there were tears coming down his face," said Dolch. "And he just started holding his head and I shook him. I needed to try to wake him up."

Dolch kept her own wits about her. She told the children, "Be responsible for each other. You know how to do that."

They obeyed her, as they filed out onto the street. There was a highway between them and the safety of Battery Park. School faculty and staff stopped traffic to get the kids safely across. Just then, they heard a thunderous, rumbling crash as one of the towers collapsed into itself. As it fell, it pushed an engulfing wave of pulverize concrete, dust and debris toward them.

Dolch, the last one to leave the school, was taking up the rear.

"All I remember is looking back and all I could see was a tsunami wave of dust and debris just coming after us," she recalled. "There was such intensity coming behind it, but it just kept rolling. My glasses were filling up. I couldn't see. And I could just feel the debris on my tongue. It was awful. It was just heavy, thick ash, so thick you could chew it."

Fortunately, most of the students were safely in the park when the building came down. Chaos erupted as the air filled with debris.

"That's when people started screaming and running, and people were getting pushed," said Dolch. "I remember seeing a park bench with a fence behind it and a tree, and I said, 'That's where I am going.' And in my heels, I jumped that fence. I don't know how I did it."

Thanks to Dolch's cool-headed leadership, all 500 of her students made it out of the building, physically unscathed. Emotionally, they will bear the scars forever, as will Dolch. What makes her story even more remarkable is that she was able to commandeer a grand-scale evacuation without losing her focus, even though she knew her sister, Wendy, was working in an upper-story office in the World Trade Center.

Wendy was one of the 700 employees of Cantor Fitzgerald who never made it out.

"I remember saying, 'God, you have to, oh my God, my sister's there. My Wendy's there,'" she remembered sadly. "I remember saying, 'God, you have to take care of her. I can't.'"

She was to find out later that her sister was among the casualties that day. While she couldn't take care of her, she could take care of her charge, 500 students, faculty and staff. And she did so with a quiet heroism.

"If you were to see my building, you'd see it standing tall. There's no coincidence that the name of our school is Leadership and Public Service. It couldn't be a coincidence."

# THANK YOU, BROTHER

THEY SAY THE HEART of a fireman is hard to know—except perhaps by another firefighter. The career is a calling, almost religious in nature. Some men wait, patiently for years until their name comes to the top of the list of candidates, so they can finally be considered for the work of their heart. Firefighters develop extraordinary devotion to others who share their calling. There's something about working with others under dangerous conditions that forges an intense bond. It's an initiation into a brotherhood, one that extends to every firefighter everywhere.

Willie Beattie has the calling. The then17-year-old was barely old enough to shave, but he'd rather spend his days at the Bryans Road Volunteer Fire Department in Maryland than finish out his senior year at the local high school. On September 11th, he was staring out the window of his classroom at the cloudless sky. He went to a firefighting class after school let out and then dropped by the firehouse. When he saw a list of others who had volunteered to go to New York to help the rescue effort, he signed right up.

The crew left late in the afternoon on Engine 112, the station's newest truck. They headed up Interstate 95 and drove straight to lower Manhattan. Once there, the Bryans Road volunteers lined up in a long queue of firefighters, all of them waiting their turn to go into the pile and look for survivors. They were one of hundreds of out-of-state fire departments that responded to the New York disaster. "It's just brothers helping brothers," said Daniel Russell, another Maryland volunteer firefighter.

The Bryans Road Team arrived just in time to help pull a surviving police officer from the debris. "Everybody was clapping. He was being carried on a stretcher and he was giving everybody a thumbs up and saying, 'Thank you,
thank you' to everyone down the line," said Beattie.

On the line, there wasn't much talk. The work was backbreaking, hauling chunks of steel and concrete dust into large steel buckets. It was heartbreaking, as well.

"I've never been to hell, but that must have looked like it," said Mike Hedges. The 28-year-old Bryans Road firefighter found the arm of a woman among the debris. It was her left arm, with a shining gold ring on her finger.

But they were rewarded with gratitude from the New York rescue workers. "They would just say, 'Thank you, brother,'" said Hedges. "The thank yous, they just sent chills up and down my spine."

"One of them turned to me and shook my hand, and he said, 'How's it going brother? My name is Marco,'" remembered Beattie. "They were so nice. If you stumbled, one of them would be there to catch you."

There was also hope that first day after the disaster that more survivors would be found. The rescuers got excited every time they uncovered office furniture and supplies that were still intact, because these might signal an air pocket where someone could have survived. But their hopes didn't pan out. After two days, local rescue workers thanked the Bryans Road crew and told them to head home.

Hedges felt unsettled afterward. About the only thing that brought him comfort was to wave an American flag at cars that passed the station house in Maryland. Sometimes, drivers would blare their horns in accord.

"It just makes me feel better to sit here and do this," he said.

## NONE DARE CALL HIM HERO

IT'S THE ONES he couldn't save who haunt Lt. Col. Paul Ted Anderson. Never mind that at least five people owe their lives to his quick thinking and fearlessness. Anderson, who had served as a paratrooper for 17 years before coming to work in the Army's Office of the Chief of Legislative Liaison, was in his Pentagon office when he heard the news about commercial airliners crashing into the World Trade Center. He had a gut feeling that the Pentagon was next, and headed down to the nearest security point to ask the guards to alert their supervisors and upgrade security.

A little after 9:30 a.m., he took a call from his wife, a sixth-grade teacher in Fayetteville, NC. She told him her students had heard what had happened and asked him to talk to them about it. He was cautioning the children not to jump to conclusions about who might be behind the attacks, when he heard a loud roar and felt the building shake. The ceiling started to cave in. The lights went out.

"There's been a bombing," he told his wife. "I've got to go."

American Airlines Flight 77 had just slammed into the southwestern corner of the Pentagon.

The then-41-year-old father of two ran into the hallway and screamed for everyone to evacuate. Military experience had taught Anderson to get out quickly, because of the likelihood of a second explosion. He ran through an emergency exit into the parking lot, corralling about 50 people to safety. Then he headed toward the noise and heat. As he ran toward the debris, two strangers joined him. One was a civilian, the other an Army sergeant. They would become an impromptu rescue team.

Anderson saw the chunks of steel from the plane and found the spot where the jet had torn a 100-foot hole in the building. Thick black smoke poured out of the hole. Fire licked the floors surrounding the crash. As the fire spread, it engulfed a Pentagon fire truck and began igniting Pentagon supply tanks full of propane and aviation fuel.

The three men picked two women off the ground and dragged them to the rescue workers about 100 yards away. Another officer found a window that had been blown out, and the men busted out the rest of the glass so they could crawl through. The smoke inside was so thick they had to crawl on the floor, keeping a hand on the adjoining wall to maintain their bearings. Inside, they found a woman in shock. She was wedged against a wall and had to be freed. They were able to drag her to an exit to other rescuers. They also carried another woman outside.

The trio reentered the building and started hollering to see whom else might need assistance. A car explosion knocked Anderson to the floor. When he got up, he saw a huge ball of flame flash past him. It was a man; the whole front of his body was on fire. Anderson and the sergeant threw themselves on him to extinguish the fire. As they dragged him to safety, the man kept yelling, "There are people behind me in the corridor! Get the people out behind me."

Anderson and the sergeant went back in again, but firemen grabbed them and pulled them out. They wouldn't let the pair re-enter—no matter how vigorously Anderson argued—because it was too dangerous. This was agonizing for him, and completely against his code of ethics.

"The military code that we live by states that if my brother, my comrade, is injured and on the battlefield, you never leave him. If I have to give my life, I will give my life, but I cannot leave my buddy behind, " he said. He was so intent on going back in, he had to be physically restrained.

"It tasted and sounded and smelled like combat," he later told a reporter. "You heard cries and screams of agony of combat. I knew people needed to be pulled off the battlefield. And we couldn't do it. That is a very bad thing to live with."

He was still onsite a few hours later, when he was asked to take a group of firefighters into the National Military Command Center, considered the Pentagons "nerve center." Their mission was to make sure the area was secure, and that air quality and temperatures were safe for the military personnel stationed there to guard the area, as well as the computer networks. He felt a moment of fear, because he didn't know what he'd find inside. But he strapped on an oxygen tank and took a respirator and headed in. He didn't think to ask for a fire helmet, coat or gloves. Fortunately, the area was secure.

Anderson finally left at around 6:30. His keys were still in his office, so he had to take the metro home. But he hasn't been able to put that day behind him. At night, he still thinks of the people firefighters found inside, their bodies stacked up just 25 feet from the exit.

While he may not think he did anything extraordinary that day, those who owe their lives to him and his two impromptu rescue partners no doubt see it differently.

## SOMEBODY'S GOT TO DO IT

"IT'S GRUESOME WORK," said Sgt. Ray Sheehan of the New York City's crime scene unit. It was also tedious. But day after day, hundreds of investigators went to the Fresh Kills landfill in Staten Island with a sense of purpose. There, they put on their disposable, white, protective bubble suits and hard hats, and sorted through the rubble that was once the twin towers.

They did it to provide whatever leads they could to FBI investigators. They did it to so the perpetrators of the September 11th attacks could be brought to justice. They did it to help families get closure.

"I'd come up here for a year or two years if they needed me to," said Efram Negron, a narcotics detective from the South Bronx, just weeks after the 9/11 disaster. He was committed to doing what it took to help.

It took about 12 hours for the crew to sift through 45,000 tons of debris. A successful find might has been a body part, melted credit cards, a wallet, a piece of jewelry or any other personal item that might have identified someone who died at the World Trade Center. Early on, a large flag was found among the debris. It then was then hung over the makeshift tent village, set up at Fresh Kills, so investigators could examine the remains of the day.

Evidence was tagged, photographed, recorded and sent to the FBI for further scrutiny. Body parts were also tagged, but then placed in refrigerated trucks to be shipped to the medical examiner's office. Police escorts accompanied them to the city morgue in Manhattan. Identification and cataloging were also part of the process. The work added new meaning to the word "monotony." Investigators found that their muscles seized up and fingers cramped from standing and digging in the same position for hours at a time.

Looking for finds on the conveyor belt—pieces of metal or other personal objects hidden among the chopped-up rocks and concrete— wasn't much easier. The slow movement of the conveyor belt made people dizzy, or mesmerized them. Every 20 minutes or so, workers had to look away and adjust their vision.

Despite that, investigators on the scene were more than willing to put all their energy into the painstaking effort of sifting through the remains of two, 110-story towers. They kept themselves psyched by posting a running tally of the number of people identified as "dead" rather than "missing," thanks to their work. If you were to ask them what brought them back day after day, they'd tell you: "Somebody's got to do it."

Who would have ever thought that a melted credit card, the remains of a makeup case or a badly charred framed photograph would mean so much? But each such find "makes you work more diligently," said one investigator on the scene. Finding anything of importance helped renew the investigator's sense of mission, which was tough to sustain after hour upon hour of finding only crushed concrete or other building debris.

The work, menial as it was, was entrusted to seasoned detectives and investigators because they know what to look for and understood the importance of paying attention to small details and the best way to handle evidence.

"These truckloads of destruction are not just being brought here and dumped in a big hole. There is a process. There is protocol," said William Allee, chief of detectives in the New York Police Department.

Many who sorted through the debris at Fresh Kills did this in addition to their other investigative work. Others just volunteered their time.

Either way, they followed the same hygiene protocols. They wore respirators to reduce the risk of breathing in contaminants such as pulverized asbestos. They rinsed off their boots and cleaned their hands thoroughly after bathroom breaks, discarded the bubble suits at the end of the day and checked for scratches or abrasions from the day's work. The air at the site was tested continuously to make sure conditions were safe.

Sometimes it was tough to know whether a personal item belonged to someone living or dead. So even when someone scored a find, no one knew where it would lead.

"Did this woman drop this purse and run to safety or was she in that building and this is what is left of her?" said Rev. Michael Harmuth, an Episcopal minister who was also the FBI chaplain. The answers to such questions were delicately sought. Contacting loved ones and relaying the information about personal belongings was a sensitive task.

A wedding band, a wristwatch, a wallet had immeasurable value to surviving family members. Tragically, it was all that remained of someone they dearly loved. But it also might provide additional detail to the question of where they were on that horrific day. After a lifetime of loving them, that's a question surviving family members, lovers and friends deserve to have answered. And the heroes of Fresh Kills helped find those answers.

## "GO ON A DIET, JOHN."

HOW DO YOU SAY "thank you" to people who risked their lives to save yours? What words could be adequate? That's a question accountant John Abruzzo grappled with after September 11th.

"I've talked to each of them individually," he said. "What do you say? Thanks? What does that mean? I don't know what to say to each of them half of the time. They saved my life. I'm here today because of those guys."

'Those guys'—Phil Caffrey, Mike Ambrosio, Mike Cursi, Tony Pecora, Gerald Simpkins, Rich Capriotti, Wilson Pacheco, Peter Bitwinski and Mike Fabiano—are John Abruzzo's coworkers in the Port Authority 69th floor business office. When the time came for them to abandon their office in the north tower of the World Trade Center, they refused to leave Abruzzo behind. Abruzzo has been a quadriplegic since a 1974 driving accident.

When the evacuation began, Abruzzo moved his motorized wheelchair into the hallway. He felt a little spooked when he saw how empty it was. Then he saw his nine coworkers rush toward him, yelling for others to evacuate. They were searching for him.

"It was more or less a collective decision that they were going to bring me down one way or the other," said Abruzzo. "The evacuation procedure says [disabled] people should wait for the firefighters, but there was no discussion of leaving me behind."

The group had been through an evacuation before. When a bomb rocked the building back in 1993, it took coworkers and emergency personnel six hellish hours to carry him to safety. The Port Authority learned a lot from that experience. Afterwards, it supplied special evacuation chairs for the disabled. The lighter chairs were meant to be less cumbersome than a wheelchair. They looked like large baby strollers combined with sleds, which made it easier to slide them down the stairs.

The men knew to look for one of these chairs for John, but did not know where they were kept. They searched closets and storage areas, knowing full well that the minutes were ticking away. The fumes from the jet fuel kept getting stronger. Finally, someone located the special chair behind a stack of boxes.

Getting John's 6' 4" frame and 250-pound body secured in the chair took all of their efforts. As soon as he was securely in the chair, the nine men began their descent down the 69 flights of stairs. Down,

down, down they went, half carrying the chair at times, half pushing it at others. It was hard work. John's girth made it difficult for him to stay balanced in the chair as the group rounded the corners of the stairwell. Anytime John shifted, someone had to grab him and hold him in place so he wouldn't fall out of the chair.

At the 44th floor, the men switched from stairwells C to B, which had a lot less smoke, but was hellishly hot. Abruzzo couldn't help but notice how hard the evacuation was on his friends. "I wasn't breaking a sweat but these guys were dripping," he said. The men did stop once to get a drink from a vending machine firefighters had pried open. Then they continued on, joking with John as they went.

"Go on a diet before we have to do this again," someone teased.

The chatter ceased at the 21st floor after the men heard a firefighter's voice on a two-way radio saying, "Two is down, two is down." The south tower, Two World Trade Center, had just collapsed. They knew they had to get out fast. Firefighters, who were also racing down the stairs, stopped the men and urged them to leave Abruzzo behind. They were probably thinking they could come back for him themselves on their return trip.

"No way," insisted coworker' Tony Pecora. "John is coming with us."

When the men reached the 10th floor, firefighters told them to stop until they checked the lower floors to make sure passage was clear. The men could feel their hearts pounding through their chests.

"It felt like a lifetime," said Pecora.;

As soon as they got the all-clear signal, they swung back into action, even though the short wait made them acutely aware of how exhausted they were. Lungs burning, fighting back fear, they continued. "We were practically carrying John at this point," said coworker Mike Ambrosio. Finally, they reached the lobby. But when they tried to leave the building, its large glass doors wouldn't open. Panic set in. After all of that, now this. Just an inch or two of glass blocked their escape.

Fortunately, a firefighter outside the building noticed them. He smashed the glass, sending shards through the air. The men rushed through the mess into the cool air. Relief hit like a brick wall. They relaxed for a moment, enough to feel their burning muscles and cramping legs. "We just dropped John," said Mike Cursi.

Then they realized they weren't yet out of harm's way. The north tower was far from stable. So the men rallied and started wheeling their friend west. They were five blocks away when the tower came down on itself at 10:28 a.m. They had been outside less than 10 minutes. It had taken them 80 minutes to evacuate, which gives Abruzzo pause.

"If any of the things happened the way they did in 1993, we wouldn't have made it. If the stairways had been more crowded, if we didn't have the evacuation chair, forget about it."

How do you say thank you to men like that?

Abruzzo doesn't know whether he'll ever find the right words. But he does know he'll spend the rest of his life trying.

# TWIST OF FATE

MIKE SHEPHERD HAD long dreamed of being a fireman. He came from a long line of firefighters, including his grandfather and great-grandfather. In 1987, he put his name on two candidate waiting lists. Then he waited. And waited. And waited.

It took more than a decade for his name to rise high enough on the list for him to be considered. Then, in the spring of 1998, he received his call. He was ecstatic. He was also confident. Shepherd scored 100 on his physical exam and 98 on the written test, making him a veritable shoe-in for the opening.

Or was he?

Now that the wait was over, there was one more hurdle to get past: Dr. Kerry Kelly, the chief medical officer of the Fire Department of New York. He watched her eyes as she went over the X-ray of his right ankle. He had had a small metal plate inserted there years before because of an old softball injury.

"Whaddya think, doc?" Shepherd asked anxiously.

She tapped the X-ray and looked directly at him

"I think you should try a different profession," she said. FDNY regulations forbid any metal in the body. So he was disqualified. He was crestfallen. After all those years. But he quickly shrugged it off. Rather than let himself be discouraged, Shepherd left the office determined that this was not the end. Not yet. Quitting was not in his vocabulary.

He knew about not giving up. Shepherd was a two time boxing champion. As an amateur boxer back in 1991 and 1992, he had belted his way to the heavyweight and lightweight Golden Gloves championships at Madison Square Garden. He had a large letter "S" for Superman tattooed on his chest. He felt he had to live up to it.

After Shepherd left Kelly's office, he made an appointment with the surgeon who had put the plate into his ankle. He told the surgeon he wanted it out by the next week. Nine weeks later, he was back in Kelly's office.

"I took my new X-ray with the plate out and my boxing jump rope with me and started skipping rope," he said with a grin." He was hired on the spot.

On September 11th, Shepherd was off duty. He was doing freelance ironwork uptown at Carnegie Hall shortly after the first plane hit the north tower of the World Trade Center.

"When I heard the second plane hit the Trade Center, I ran out into the streets and thought about my real job," he said. He hitched a ride on a fire truck stuck in traffic a few blocks away from where he was working. Once he reached the site, he scanned the area. Looking up at the towers, he sensed trouble.

"As soon as I got to Ground Zero, I knew from working high iron that those buildings were going to come down," he said.

Perhaps it was the hand of fate at work, perhaps it was divine intervention, but his rescue efforts brought him face-to-face with Dr. Kelly that day. She and a fire captain had located several injured people under six inches of soot, and she needed his help. Together, they got the injured people to a parking garage. Shepherd ripped off his shirt, soaked it with a fire hose and helped clean away the matted blood from one of the injured firefighters, so Kelly could see the source of the wound. Kelly knew that the man needed hospital care.

And it was clear they needed other medical supplies. Shepherd, now bare-chested, with his "S" tattoo readily visible, helped Kelly find those supplies. They carefully picked through the surreal moonscape that was once the financial district. At one point, Shepherd tensed with fear. In a flash, he grabbed Kelly by her arm and pulled her away from the building she was about to enter.

"I told her that the second tower was about to come down," he remembered with a shudder. Had she entered that building, she could have lost her life beneath the debris. By the time the deafening rumble filled the air, Shepherd and Kelly were a safe distance away.

"It was so strange," Kelly said later. "Here was this guy in the smoke and the dust with no shirt and a big letter 'S' on his chest, a subliminal message that Superman had arrived." They parted shortly afterwards so each could go where they were most needed, but she later met up with him again. She embraced him warmly. "You saved my life, Mike," she said.

She had thought about that day three years before, when she told Shepherd to find a new career. And she wondered. If he had not persisted, would there have been another Mike Shepherd by her side that day to pull her out of harm's way?

"Boy, am I happy that I was wrong about him," she said. "He was amazing. Mike did a great job down there all day. So did all the firefighters. It was the worst day in our history—and our finest.

# WORKING THE MOUND

THE RESCUE WORKERS at Ground Zero weren't the only ones who toiled like dogs, putting in grueling 12-hour days on what has come to be known as "the mound." They had plenty of help from some 350 loyal, obedient dogs, trained to assist in rescue and search operations.

The dogs—mostly German shepherds and black or yellow Labrador retrievers—and their handlers came from all over: Connecticut, Iowa, Miami, Mississippi, even Europe. It was said to be the largest deployment ever of rescue dogs. Some were trained to find people who are still alive, others to find corpses or human remains. Fire and police departments have used them for years because a dog's sense of smell is far more sensitive than a human's. They can pick up scents even through concrete.

The dogs are also perfect for getting into small spaces, moving through debris that an average sized-man couldn't get through. At one point, Cara, a 2-year-old Beauceron herding dog, tunneled 40 feet with a small camera strapped around her neck. She was looking for remains.

At Ground Zero, those skills proved incredibly useful. Porkchop, an Australian shepherd with a blond silky coat, found enough human remains, plus wallets and purses, to help investigators identify four people.

The training is grueling. Dogs are taught to override their basic instincts, which is hard for any creature. They learn to run without digging in their claws, as they normally would, because normal behavior could create a landslide on fragile mounds of debris. They're trained to keep their paws spread apart without disturbing anything in their path—and to stay put when the ground moves unexpectedly, even though their instinct may be to jump. This prepares them to assist in areas where there have been earthquakes or building collapses. They're also trained to stay calm amidst mayhem. Screaming, people rushing from a scene and earth-moving equipment do not faze them.

Cadaver dogs are trained using donated placenta and cadavers or such products as Pseudo Corpse, which emits a smell like decomposing flesh. The Federal Emergency Management Agency sets rigorous standards for these dogs.

"The dogs are wonderful," said Nishi Dhupa, director of emergency and critical care at the Cornell Hospital for Animals in New

York. She set up the emergency tent, which was initially on the frontline, and managed the emergency treatment and care of the dogs. They needed that kind of care because they worked the "hot spots" on the mountainous piles of rubble, places where fires burning deep within made movement perilous.

Many of the dogs suffered from heat stroke and exhaustion, plus serious physical injuries from the sharp shrapnel and precarious positioning of the melted beams and other dangerous debris. Others required hydration from intravenous fluids.

"We tried to talk to the handlers to let us keep the dogs on IV fluids, but they were anxious to get back to the mound," said Dhupa.

"When the dogs come off their shift on 'the mound,' as everyone calls it, we check their footpads for debris and lacerations and wash their eyes with a special solution, then do a quick medical exam," she said. "If the dogs are covered with debris, we have a makeshift shower with a bucket and a hose to decontaminate and cool them down."

A specialist in emergency veterinary care at disaster scenes, Dhupa originally brought supplies and equipment from the New York State College of Veterinary Medicine, when she reported for duty on Sept. 17. A first-aid tent and mobile veterinary hospital were set up near the site. Since then, she has been caring for the trained dogs, trying to keep them together in body and mind. And yes, the dogs have gotten depressed.

"These dogs are trained to find live people—it's positive energy for them— but they're just finding cadavers and body parts," she said. "The handlers try to stay upbeat, because the dogs take cues from them, even though they [the handlers] are very upset and are moved to tears. Sometimes the handlers hide, so the dogs can find them. We also give them affection. The handlers are bringing dogs back to get cuddled and the dogs are really perking up when that happens."

When Porkchop came for routine checks at the medical station, for instance, he was rewarded with a kiss on the snout, a scratch on the tummy and plenty of heartfelt encouragement to retain his upbeat mood. "What a good boy, Porkchop!"

During his break time, he got to watch *Animal Planet*, crack acorns and eat ants. There were enough dog bones, chew toys and doggie biscuits to quality the VMAT as doggie heaven.

But even when the dogs became dispirited by their lack of 'finds,' their presence has been positive for the humans working the mound.

"They're providing therapy for all of us," said Dhupa. "People like to talk to them. There's a positive feedback thing going on at the mound," she said.

Certainly the rescue workers needed it. Blizzard, who sifted through the rubble with Connecticut State Trooper Stowell Burnham, helped him find a child's shoe and a photograph of someone's family.

"It was the saddest, crudest sight you could ever imagine," he said. "These were working people. It definitely affects you."

The dogs are Ground Zero have given so much, it breaks your heart. Eager to please, they don't stop until their handlers are ready to stop. Some of the dogs, such as 9-year-old Judd, collapsed with heat stroke. All the dogs were exhausted. The conditions were bad enough to prompt a pharmaceutical company to donate nebulizer medications to help the dogs breathe easier. Rockefeller University located a supply of doggie goggles to protect the animals' eyes. But most of the search-and-rescue dogs had trouble getting used to the eyewear. Still, they kept searching.

"Our primary mission is to get people out," said Michael Kidd, a then-36-year-old member of the Miami Dade Fire Rescue team, who brought his German shepherd, Mizu. "But what's important here is a sense of closure for the families."

The dogs helped investigators provide that for some. Although they couldn't provide that for everyone, it wasn't from the dogs' lack of trying.

# IT'S A GRAND OLD FLAG

IF YOU CAN'T HELP—although you desperately want to—you can at least express solidarity.

That thought came to Paul Morgan, a Charles County, MD, sheriff's detective, and he followed it through to its natural conclusion. Morgan remembered that he had a flag-like canvas in his attic that might be perfect as the backdrop. The 3' by 5' large white rectangle sported a red, white and blue Statue of Liberty. The word "LIBERTY" was emblazoned across it. Morgan had displayed it during Fourth of July celebrations in the past.

But now he envisioned it covered with the encouraging words of other law enforcement and rescue personnel. Soon after he got his inspiration, Morgan contacted all the local fire and police departments in the area as well as emergency workers, and asked them to sign their names on the coarse canvas, with their prayers and well wishes. He knew that they—like him—felt badly about not being invited to help with the rescue efforts. The canvas would give them an opportunity to contribute. He spent about a week bringing it around the community so others could sign it.

Morgan then drove to the Pentagon, and asked rescue and recovery workers there to add their thoughts and prayers, as well.

"This is a show of support," said Tom Swann, a La Plata, MD, volunteer firefighter who signed the flag along with 30 others. "So many of us wanted to be there. You can look into the eyes of the people at the Pentagon and then the workers at the World Trade Center and you can see it's the same thing, the same emotions," he said.

After Morgan had collected all the signatures he could, he packed it up, took some friends along for the ride and headed north to the remains of the World Trade Center.

Patrick Lynch, president of the New York Patrolmen's Benevolent Association, accepted the signed canvas on behalf of the rescue workers, clearly touched.

"We've gotten a huge amount of support from around the country," said Lynch. "But this is the first symbolic gesture. There's a bond between the rescue workers here in New York and those at the Pentagon."

What was once a novelty item had become a symbol of the bonds uniting north and south and law and rescue workers everywhere. That sense of unity was one of the best things to come out of September 11th.

But Morgan wasn't the only one from Maryland inspired to bring a tangible symbol of support to New York. The folks at the Fort McHenry National Monument, the place where the Battle of Baltimore was waged in 1812 and where Francis Scott Key was inspired to write "The Star Spangled Banner," decided to give New York the fort's historic flag. They said they hoped it would wave atop the memorial that will be built to honor those who died at the World Trade Center. Sen. Charles Schumer (D-NY) accepted it on behalf of his constituents.

"It will remind us that the nation is behind us, and it will help us rebuild," he said.

# HEALERS, COMFORTERS, SUSTAINERS

## LOVE LETTERS STRAIGHT FROM THE HEART

You could say they were just a bunch of letters. Some were written with incomplete or run-on sentences. Some words were misspelled. Some carried the unmistakable markings of preteen girls: the letter 'i' dotted with round, open circles and hearts or smiley faces drawn next to their names. But in their imperfection lay their charm. They were sent from children around the country to encourage and thank the rescue workers at the Pentagon and World Trade Center.

"I'm sorry if you lost someone you loved," wrote then-fifth-grader Susan McLaughlin of the Good Shepherd Parochial School in Gerritsen Beach, Brooklyn, NY. "But look what you're doing for everyone in America."

The first batch arrived in large plastic buckets, along with hygiene essentials like toothbrushes and soap for the rescue workers. Volunteers posted them where workers could see them. By the end of the night, word of them had spread, and many beaten-down rescue workers stopped by to read their heartfelt messages. They were in need of something to refresh their souls after days of finding only body parts, instead of survivors. The letters did the trick.

"Dear firefighters and police officers, thank you for working hard to save people," read one letter. It was written on orange construction paper with crayon drawings of an American flag and flowers. "You are our heroes. We are proud of you. Love, Patty."

"I hope this isn't a bad time to read a letter from an 11-year-old," wrote one middle-school student. "If I were in your shoes, I wouldn't want to be a rescuer. Anyway do you have any children? If you do, go spend time with them." Then he added, "I think you should go back to your job now and rescue more people."

"Dear heroes," wrote another student. "Thank you for saving New York City. My grandma was there. I really appreciate it. Love, Jesse."

Brooklyn firefighter Joe Williams, weary from the search-and-rescue effort, stopped to look at the letters as the sun set that first Saturday after the disaster. He said tears welled up in his eyes.

Rescue workers at the Pentagon were also moved. "As we read the letters, we passed them around," said Charlie Allen, a rescue worker volunteering at the Pentagon cleanup. "Then the whole tent got into it. We were real involved in what we were doing. When we finally got to sit down and take a breath, it kind of broke a lot of guys up. It's one thing to do your job. It's another thing to sit back and hear it from a 10-year-old."

Some rescue workers even took the time to write back to the children. "In this time of sadness, it was your letter that kept me going each night," Army Sgt. David Andino wrote to one sixth-grader in Virginia. "I carry your letter in my pocket every day, so if I need cheering up I know someone cares."

Letters like that helped the students realize how much good they had done by writing the letters. "This was so big that a lot of people must think that kids can't do anything to help," said 11-year-old letter writer Alex Darr. "The letters were just a little thing. But they made a big difference."

Indeed.

"Some people call us heroes," wrote firefighter Carl Mauney. "America is made up of lots of heroes. I think all types of jobs are important. For you students, sending the thank you cards was the right thing to do. It took time and concentration. In my mind, that makes you heroes."

# WHAT OKLAHOMA CITY UNDERSTOOD

NO ONE IS BETTER QUALIFIED to comfort those whose loved ones have died suddenly, under violent circumstances, than someone who has already been through it. So who could better understand the pain of the families in the New York area than those who lost loved ones in the April 19, 1995, bombing of the Alfred Murray Federal Building?

"I was driving to Tulsa to visit my father that morning when I heard about the World Trade Center on the radio," said Diane Leonard, whose husband was killed in the Oklahoma City explosion. "I knew those families would be dealing with so much grief."

"I remember thinking, 'Maybe there's something we can give that no one else can.'" She started calling around to local and state organizations. Little did she know that Ken Thompson, who had lost his wife that same day, was doing the same. He also wanted to give something back. "So many people reached out to us six years ago from all over the country," he said.

The Oklahoma City National Memorial Institute for the Prevention of Terrorism referred both of them to the American Red Cross. Organizers there arranged for them to provide counseling at New York's Family Assistance Center at Pier 94.

"We told them our story, how we got through, how we survived," said Thompson. "We gave them a chance to talk to someone who has been through something similar."

Leonard and Thompson proved to be such a source of comfort that the American Red Cross worked with its Oklahoma City office to coordinate a continuous flow of volunteers from among those Oklahoma City survivors who were emotionally ready to talk about their experience and provide comfort to others.

One of them was Kathleen Treanor, whose 4-year-old daughter was with her in-laws visiting the Social Security office that day at the Alfred Murray Federal Building.

"I miss my daughter dreadfully every day," said Treanor. Yet, she was determined to make sure that her daughter's death was not in vain. "Her light shines for me. She's not really gone. My sharing of her can offer other people some comfort."

Treanor counseled families in New York, too, but her compassion drove her to talk to rescue workers as well. "You can see the pain and weariness in their eyes, the horror of what they've seen," she said. "It breaks your heart because you know what lies ahead for them." She encouraged the families of the victims to reach out to each other and the rescue workers. She knew that sharing would help ease their loss.

"When you are suffering, the best thing you can do is reach out to help others who are suffering," she said.

Yet counseling came with a price for the volunteers. They knew that going to New York would rip open the old wounds. They'd touch that place of heartbreaking loss once again.

"Yes, we do relive our losses, in a way, when we talk to the New York City victims," said Thompson, "But I am so thankful to have the ability to help others. Nothing could be more rewarding."

# 21 NURSES

THEY WERE 21 NURSES. Most of them had just finished an exhausting 12- hour shift at a hospital in Washington, DC. On a normal day, they would have had some breakfast, gone to bed at 10 a.m., and then gotten up in time to go back to work. These nurses were working a four- to six-week rotation for Fastaff, a Denver-based nursing placement agency.

But on the morning of September 11th, they got off duty and went straight to the office of Andre 'Shep' Shepart, the operations manager for the regional office of Fastaff. He was surprised to see them. They asked him whether they could grab a ride with him to the Pentagon. He had just seen a TV broadcast about the plane crash at the Pentagon, so he said yes. The nurses who couldn't fit in the company shuttle walked several blocks on foot.

Shepart was impressed. "Many of them had been up for at least one day, some two days, on their feet and working, and they still walked over to the Pentagon," he said.

Nurse Carol Morgan was one of them. The Oklahoma native was an oncology nurse and a minister. She'd been fast asleep when American Airlines Flight 77 crashed into the Pentagon.

"My roommate had knocked on my door and woke me up," said Morgan. "We threw on our clothes and got as close as we could to the site, when we saw Shep in the van with the other nurses." Morgan joined the staff at the scene.

Their timing was perfect. The nurses arrived as the first-and only—wave of the injured were brought in. One man, totally covered in jet fuel, was near hysteria. The nurses had to calm him down and help wash him off.

"Boy, were those doctors in the triage units happy to see our staff," Shepart said. "They had no real use for the untrained people who were stand- mg around hoping to help. They needed medical people."

The nurses stayed until early evening, logging well over 24 hours on active duty. Some stayed until early the next morning, even traveling with the burn victims to the hospital, where they worked to make sure they received good care.

"I was so proud of them. It wasn't easy to be there," said Shepart. "I am retired from the air force, and this felt like the real thing, the thing we had trained for. People were hysterical. All the while, we kept hearing alarming reports about another plane coming, another attack. And there were our nurses, all dog-tired, all doing their best in a national emergency. They are just an amazing caliber of people."

No doubt the work was hard on them. Their exhaustion made them even more emotionally susceptible to the pain of the victims.

Carol Morgan still can't speak of September 11th without crying, and she faces death and despair on a daily basis.

"I was devastated and I still just get real teary," she said. "Usually I can separate myself from the suffering very easily. But that day, well, that day it was hard. I guess because it wasn't so much medicine as we know it. It was that we didn't know what was in front of us. We couldn't control what was going to happen. It was just chaos."

For her, the day was eerily reminiscent of another day years before, when she was attending to the wounded outside the bombed federal building in Oklahoma.

"The Oklahoma City bombing was one thing," she said. "This was entirely different. I guess because it was a direct attack on us, as a nation, on our government. This felt like it cut right to the core of our hearts. There were more deaths and it was happening right in front of me."

As she grappled with her emotions while working in the triage unit, some special energy inside her kicked in and gave her the power to keep going. Whatever it was, it connected her to the firemen and the rescue workers and everyone who was there to do a job.

"It felt like adrenaline," she said. "You know, it was the sprit of the Lord and when it flows, it flows fast. And you just know what you have to do."

And so it was for the other 20 nurses. Sacrificing sleep, pushing their own bodies to the brink of exhaustion, these angels of mercy did what needed to be done.

# SOMETHING TO CUDDLE WITH

KIRSTIN SHIPP KNEW what it was like to lose a parent. The Washington, DC, native, who was 12 on 9/11, had lost her father when she was only 3.

So when she learned that children had lost their own parents in the terrorist attacks, she couldn't help but feel their loss. She desperately wanted to reach out to them. But how?

Then it came to her.

"They need something to cuddle with," said Kirstin. "I know I'd need something to cuddle with."

Kirstin was a big fan of stuffed animals. *The Velveteen Rabbit* by Margery Williams, a story about a stuffed animal that desperately wants to become real—and does so through the power of love—is one of her favorite books. She had a special bond with her own stuffed animals. She told them her problems, hugged them and loved them—which she thought was pretty much what those kids needed right then.

So she sprung into action. Kirstin knew how to make things happen. When she was 9, she felt compelled to help the children left homeless after a tornado ripped through a small town in Oklahoma. She fretted over the fact that the kids didn't have any possessions. So she launched a book drive and solicited help from everyone, including the mayor and the American Red Cross. She collected over 10,000 books for the kids who didn't have any.

The contacts she made at the Red Cross in 1999 eased the way for her new initiative, Stuffed Animals for Healing and Comfort. Over 5,000 stuffed animals poured into her house and into collection boxes placed at stores and public offices around town. But she just couldn't let the plush pets go out so impersonally.

The then-seventh-grader painstakingly attached a tag to each one, with a special message for the child who would be hugging it later that week, which the Red Cross distributed to the families of the victims.

The note read: "Hi, my name is Kirstin Shipp and I'm 12 years old. I'm very sorry you lost someone you love. This animal comes to heal and comfort and in time, to help your smile return. Love, Kirstin."

# DOCTORS AND NURSES ON THE FRONT LINE

*On the utmost brink we stood,*
*And like the winds of some unresting wood*
*The gathered murmur from those depths of woe*
*Soughed upward into thunder.*
*Out from this*
*The unceasing sound comes ever. I might not tell*
*How deep the Abyss down sank from hell to hell,*
*It was so clouded and so dark no sight*
*Could pierce it.*

*--Dante's Inferno*

WHEN DANTE WROTE his depiction of hell back in the 13th century, he could not have guessed how much it would apply to Sept. 11, 2001.

Dr. Tom Mayer, chairman of the department of emergency medicine at Inova Fairfax Hospital in Fall Church, VA, saw the parallel immediately.

"How did Dante know what the inside of Pentagon would look like?" he asked. "But he did."

"We saw things thing we did not want to see, we heard things we did not want to hear," said Mayer, who played a key role in coordinating medical care at the Pentagon. "We heard things we did not want to hear. We smelled things we did not want to smell. We thought thoughts we did not want to think."

In Washington and New York, doctors and nurses who thought they had seen it all— who thought nothing could shock them anymore—were just as shaken by the events as everyone else.

In New York, physicians, nurses, even medical school and pre-med students, came rushing to the World Trade Center as soon as they heard the news. Among them was Middletown, NY, internist Raymond Basri, who arrived moments after the second tower fell. He said it looked like "a nuclear winter."

"Everything and everyone at Ground Zero was covered in gray ash," said Dr. Joseph Ornato, medical director for Richmond (VA) Ambulance Authority. He was in New York for a meeting, and followed a fire department lieutenant to the World Trade Center, where he helped set up a triage site and temporary morgue. "It was as if all the color had been drained out of the world."

Amidst the chaos, the uncertainty, the horrible acrid odor, doctors and nurses kept working. They helped burn victims, treated lacerations, irrigated damaged eyes and assisted rescuers with respiratory problems that came from breathing in the dust, insulation, asbestos and jet fuel fumes.

"The dust would turn to concrete in their eyes," said Dr. Anthony Gordon, a radiologist who drove the 871 miles through the night from Georgia so he could volunteer his help. We'd rinse them out with saline, force them to rest a bit and then they would go back out. Like everyone, I wish I could have done more."

The medical personnel on the front line put themselves in as much danger as the rescue workers. But Dr. Ornato of Richmond was careful not to characterize them as heroes. "The real heroes are the men and women who were the first there and who were willing to go into harm's way to help their fellow man," he said.

Meanwhile, medical teams at hospitals throughout New York, Connecticut and New Jersey braced themselves for the onslaught that never came. Janice Latham, an emergency room nurse at Cornell Presbyterian, waited for hours, then got so frustrated she marched down toward the disaster site. She was stopped by a New York police officer.

Latham tried to argue her way past the barriers.

"I want to be helping people. I've got years of experience," she said.

But he wouldn't budge. "We're not even letting emergency personnel in there. You can't get close enough."

"But I'm trained in burns. I can do something for these people," she responded.

"I don't think you can," he said, with bitterness in his voice. Then he turned her away.

He may have been right. For the most part, there was only one wave of survivors after the collapse of the Twin Towers. After that, the people who showed up to receive medical care were the rescue workers who gave their all under very dangerous conditions.

Dr. Robert Lahita, a physician and head of Hudson County Emergency Services, coordinated the establishment of field clinics and command centers 1 at Liberty State Park, the Holland Tunnel and Exchange Place Pier. For the first few hours, he treated about 100 people, fixing triage tags on them: green for not badly injured, yellow for worse injuries, red for critical and black for dead. After the initial rush, he warned his nurses, "Be prepared. You'll probably see things you never saw before."

But they didn't see another patient for hours.

And they never saw another survivor.

"This is something you cannot imagine," he said. "Ten hours after it happened, you couldn't get close enough to help."

# ABOUNDING GRACE'S MOTORCYCLE MINISTER

THE REV. RICHARD DEL RIO Del Rio was one of the first clergymen to arrive at Ground Zero after the planes hit and the towers caught fire. He caught the news on television, slapped on his collar and rode his motorcycle downtown.

The pastor of Abounding Grace Church is experienced at "street ministry." He founded the evangelical church in 1982 to minister to prostitutes, drug addicts, the homeless, wayward kids and the incarcerated. "We wanted to reach the people that no one wants," he said.

But even 20 years of working in the most hard-core situations did not prepare him for what he saw. "I can't describe it. I've been to the poorest countries, I'd seen devastation before, but this was like a war zone," he recalled. And it wasn't just contained neatly in a small space—it went on for 20 or 30 city blocks."

As soon as he arrived, the police were only too happy to put him to work. They know him well. Del Rio has served the New York City Police Department as a clergy liaison, mediating on their behalf when there are gang- related problems.

One police officer grabbed him and asked him to do last rites on body parts covered in plastic. He did that, and whatever else was needed, including cleaning out a van that was thick with gritty ash so it could be used to transport bodies to the morgue, and cleaning up the entrance to the Brooks Brothers store, which was being used for medical triage. It didn't matter what he did. His presence made a difference.

"As a preacher you usually have answers—you're proactive," said Del Rio. You're used to saying something," he said. "But this time, I was at a total loss for words. This was a time that I just had to be there. Firefighters, policemen, they saw me and looked at me as the closest link to God. Father Judge was already dead and I was the only visible clergy. I heard men say to me, 'We need more like you.' I was there to be an ear. That really blew me away."

In the days that followed, Del Rio became a common fixture at the scene. He quickly recognized the need for more clergy. So, making use of his connections with the police department and many pastors in the evangelical community, he organized the Ground Zero Clergy Task Force. He was gratified to see it come together because it created unity where none had been.

"The evangelical church has pretty much been fragmented and hasn't worked together well," he explained. "This has been the chance to overcome this glaring deficiency. From this event, immediately God just sort of worked it out. We have been training, working with local clergy to get their credentials with the police department so they can have access during these times."

The Ground Zero Clergy task force gave more men and women of the cloth the opportunity to provide the spiritual support sorely needed at the disaster site. There were many who struggled to understand how a merciful God could let such a terrible thing happen.

Del Rio isn't one of them. He sees God's hand behind the fact that more lives were spared than taken at the World Trade Center. The operable question for him isn't, "God, how could you let this happen?"

"It isn't that at all," he said. "I see evil all the time. We live in an evil area with bad people doing bad things. This is really an example, a devastating one, of the degradation of men who are following an evil path. I look at this and think, there could have been 50,000 people in there. There weren't. It is a miracle that more people did not die, that there was not more far-reaching devastation."

But even Del Rio is struck by the immensity of the tragedy.

"This is devastation, such massive devastation, that I am still in awe that this could happen," he said.

Given that, how is he to help those who are struggling with their faith in the wake of the events?

"I don't have to say a whole lot. I listen, I pray for them and their families. I deal."

# THERE TO FIND THE HAND OF GOD

IT DIDN'T MATTER that most of the devastation took place 3,000 miles away on the opposite side of the country. Fire Captain John White, chaplain for the Los Angeles City Fire Department and president of Firefighters for Christ, knew he had to go to Ground Zero to help. He arrived a few days after September 11th.

Officially, he was part of a stress-debriefing unit, organized to help the rescuers cope during the long, arduous days of tiring and emotionally devastating work. But his real mission was to make Christ's presence palpable to those struggling with their own grief and loss. He came cross-country to find the hand of God in what transpired, and to help his fellow firefighters to grasp it.

"Amidst all this destruction, there was story after story of people escaping absolute, sure death—real miracles among all of this," he said. To him that's evidence that "God is a God of salvation. In Him alone belongs escape from death. His hand is the hand of mercy."

During his days at Ground Zero, White often prayed over the desiccated bodies of his brother firefighters. But he worked just as hard to minister to the living, praying that they might not be scarred by all they had seen.

"I have been a firefighter for 44 years," he said. "After that much time, I thought I had seen it all. But when I got to New York . . . well, it was just beyond explanation. As a firefighter, in talking with another firefighter, he knows what I am talking about," he continued. "We know each other's hearts. But I can't even explain to another firefighter what I saw. The things these men were exposed to—it's going to be devastating for them. They will lock these images into their brains from now on," he said.

He knows that from experience.

"I vividly remember a young lady I was in a process of rescuing 43 years ago," he said. "She had been totally burned, every inch of her body. I can picture her clearly. I can see her in front of me now. And I can hear her screams. If that memory is etched in my mind so many years later, how much worse will it be for them? The horrid memories they have had to contend with."

He said he was less affected by the deaths than by the suffering of the survivors.

"I've seen hundreds of people die, and almost every one of them, except for the suicides, was not expecting to die. So the thing that hurt me more than anything else, was what our guys were exposed to, trying to dig their buddies out. It was heartbreaking watching brothers look for brothers."

Each time they found a firefighter, he said, the ritual to honor him was the same. Rescuers would place the body in a long steel rectangular bucket. Then they would wrap the body in a flag. All the firefighters would form two lines. Fire Captain John White or another chaplain would pray over him.

Afterwards, the men carrying the bucket would bring it down between the lines of firefighters so each could salute him. Afterwards, the firefighter would be put in the back of an ambulance.

"And they do it again, over and over, because those are their guys, their family, their brothers," said White.

As difficult as it was, White was glad he could help. "We prayed with men, we encouraged men, we prayed over bodies that were taken out, we were there with men who wanted to invite Jesus into their hearts. We were there to try to help the city, which has had its heart ripped out of the fire service."

And even when one's heart feels ripped out, said White, there is solace to be found in the soul.

# RESCUER ONE DAY, CLERIC THE NEXT

AS COINCIDENCE WOULD HAVE IT, Lt. Col. Carl Pfeiffer, chaplain for the Fort Jackson, SC-based 1st Basic Combat Training Brigade was in Crystal City, right near the Pentagon, on September 11th. He was there to work on a special project with the Army Chief of Chaplains.

"We had to evacuate the building," he said. "When we got to the street we saw smoke coming from the Pentagon. We went over and immediately began helping out. The fire was humongous and there was wreckage everywhere," he recalled. "Firefighters and medics were already there. We'd help lift stretchers with people suffering from smoke inhalation into trucks that took them over to the triage area under a bridge."

Pfeiffer was one of the many military chaplains who joined together to set up a chaplain operations center the very next day. Chaplains were organized into teams, so they could make sure that the essential needs were met. One team, the comfort team, provided solace to the families, victims and stunned rescue workers. The mortuary team worked alongside those who pulled bodies from the rubble. They prayed for the deceased and administered last rites.

"We were there to give dignity and respect for those that died in defense of their country. We attempted to provide a profound witness for all around," he said. That included the family members who were brought to the site later that week, so they could lay memorial items for the loved ones. The chaplains knew the families needed to do that for their emotional wellbeing.

"The reason to allow them to come to the Pentagon was when they finally see the building there is a sense of closure," he said. "It helps them to accept the full dimension of the tragedy that occurred."

He said it was a privilege to be there, to listen and guide and provide hope. "It was really sacred work."

# THE CHEERLEADERS

WHEN THOMAS Peebler grabbed six men to lead a yell on the sidelines of Princeton football game in front of the student body one fine fall day in 1884, he unwittingly became the nation's first cheerleader. Propelled by the excitement of the game and an overwhelming desire to encourage his team, Peebler threw caution to the wind, raised his voice and made history.

Since then, cheerleading has been part of the fabric of America. Go watch a professional football game, or a college basketball tournament, or high school scrimmage if you aren't convinced. The urge to cheerlead is so American, New Yorkers who were fleeing for their lives from the Twin Towers began doing it spontaneously when they saw firefighters run into the buildings and up the stairwells.

"God bless you," some yelled. "Way to go." "We love you." Cheers of encouragement continued to ring out. Behind them was a desire to thank the firefighters, acknowledge their courage and give them the strength to do a difficult job. The vocal outpouring was so enthusiastic it could have raised the roof.

Through the long days of recovery that followed, the cheering continued. On the following morning, residents of New York lined the barricades that kept the world at bay so rescue workers could do their jobs. They had come simply to cheer the rescuers on.

For Jeff Cook, an NYU law student, it was a sight to behold. He left his TriBeCa apartment, to take a short run along the Hudson River on the West Side Highway.

"I was floored by what I saw. People lined the West Side Highway, for nearly a mile stretch on both sides, from barricade to barricade between Houston and 14th Street," he said. "I saw thousands of men, women and children, young and old, within the barricaded zone, brought together, waving the American flag, the symbol of hope for the free world, and cheering on the rescue teams as they continuously poured into the disaster area."

Cook said that the sound of the cheering crowds, the patriotism and the love that filled the air was deeply stirring.

"Seeing that brought tears to my eyes, as it did to those around me," he said. "In this most difficult of trials, the American spirit rises to the challenge. We have come together. We will rebuild and we will not live in fear. We remain the greatest experiment in democracy the world has ever known. God bless us all."

Tapping into that great reserve of strength and hope, the crowd gave back what it could to the rescuer workers who were giving their all.

Thomas Peebler had no idea what he had started.

# THE CANINE THERAPY CREW

YOU'VE NO DOUBT HEARD of dogs trained to sniff out survivors, or dead bodies. Many such dogs worked long days at Ground Zero. But other dogs were there to serve as canine comfort-givers. They were pioneers in what could be a new role for animals in crisis relief work. Over 100 of these specially trained animals and their owners volunteered to work at the family assistance center at Pier 94 in New York, or to accompany families taking the ferry from the pier to the World Trade Center so they could see the circumstances under which their loved ones had died.

Greer Griffith's black Labrador, Clayton, a retired seeing-eye dog, was one of the ones who worked on the ferries. On the deck, Griffith waited for the Red Cross counselor to motion to her to bring Clayton over. That's standard procedure for the dog handlers. She brought Clayton over to comfort a distraught woman.

"The woman reached out and touched Clayton, and he jumped up on the seat beside her," she recalled. "Then she hugged him and cried. I just stood there. He knew what to do."

"The dogs have worked the most wonders with men and boys, the tough type of people who don't necessarily know how to let go and show emotion," said Susan Urban, associate director of counseling at the American Society for the Prevention of Cruelty to Animals. The society has made sure that only properly certified animals participate. It also scheduled the animals.

"I oversee 175 counselors, psychologists and social workers, and I wish they all had four feet," said Margaret Pepe, the disaster mental health officer for the American Red Cross relief operation, who has been organizing counselors at the pier. "The dogs are incredibly effective. I'm jealous of the four-footed therapists and their ability to engage and relax people in a matter of minutes."

And there were several trained cats. The pets and their owners belong to a handful of pet therapy organizations, including Therapy Pet International of Flanders, NJ, the oldest and largest group, founded in 1976; the Brooklyn, NY-based Good Dog Foundation and the Seattle-area Delta Society.

There were also four dog teams from an Oregon organization called Hope, which provides special training in crisis intervention. The Oregon Red Cross flew the teams out to provide comfort to the firefighters, police officers and rescue workers at Ground Zero. Other pet handlers and their animals came from California, Colorado, Maine and New Hampshire.

Animals who are certified to provide this kind of service are trained to stay calm no matter what. They learn not to get excited even when there are sudden loud noises, or a young child yanks their tails or pulls their ears. Trainers say that takes an amazing amount of focus for a dog and can be exhausting for them.

Although the dogs are trained in pet therapy, the handlers do not claim to be therapists.

"We're only qualified to talk about our dogs and to make people smile and relax," said Mario Canzoneri, a member of Therapet in Clark, NJ. "We're not counselors or psychiatrists." The Staten Island sewer inspector and owner of two golden retrievers, Jake and Jesse, who were the first to go to Pier 94 to help those who were grieving.

The field of animal-assisted therapy is new, but the link between animals and healing is ancient. Hunter-gathers left intricate drawings depicting the link between spiritual healing and animals. Florence Nightingale recommended small pets for the chronically ill. Studies in the last 20 years show that spending time with pets can significantly reduce stress. Something about their innocence and affection just melts people and helps them to feel better.

While it is not likely that the animals that were pressed into service understood why they were needed that day, they gave love as they always do, happily wagging their tails and looking to return licks of affection for a small scratch behind the ears. What could be better than that?

## ALABAMA'S HIGH-STEPPING MARCHING BAND

THE LAST QUESTION on anyone's mind on September 12th, the day Americans woke up to an unsettling new world was: Where's the marching band?

One determined group of fife piping, drum banging, high steppers decided that the question didn't need to be asked. Good thing, because they probably would have been told No. Many a well-intentioned volunteer was turned away. There were just too many who wanted to help, and they were getting in the way of the more critical work that needed to be done.

But the small college band from Alabama didn't know any of this. All they knew was that they felt called to bring their patriotic music up north. So Dr. Anthony Paul piled the band members of the National Association for the Prevention of Starvation into their van in Huntsville, Alabama on the Thursday after the attacks without bothering to figure out where they would sleep once they arrived in Manhattan, or how much cash they'd need for the return trip. They just got in and kept driving for 24 hours. When they got to lower Manhattan, they prepped like they would for any parade. They slid on their tubas, strapped on their drums, and grasped the batons. As soon as they got there, they were ready to go.

"The minute we stepped out of the van and started playing America the Beautiful,' people started clapping and getting out of cars," said Paul. "Policemen started saluting and we started a procession. We went to St. Vincent's and played hymns for people mourning." (St. Vincent's Hospital had received most of the injured during the attacks on the Twin Towers.)

The band members got a surprise, too. They never expected New Yorkers to embrace them with such warmth and enthusiasm.

"Someone directed us to Washington Square Park," said Paul. "There were about 2,000 folks there, and the crowd parted for us and we started playing 'Amazing Grace' and people started crying. Then people directed us to Union Square." At the community squares that border lower Manhattan, candles, flowers and prayer vigils were kept for the weeks following the collapse.

The college musicians must have been riding high on the wave of patriotism because they kept going without food or rest. "We marched for eight hours without food, only water," said Paul. "Then on Sunday morning, we marched from one firehouse to another. As we approached fire stations, the firemen had gotten word we were coming from the previous fire station, and they would be out to greet us."

He said it was an unforgettable experience.

"Every place we went, it repeated itself: crying, clapping, lots of hugs," said Paul. "We told them we love them and we feel their pain and though we're from Alabama, we're all one."

# 'GOTTA DO SOMETHING'

## DIVING TO PREVENT DISASTER

$T$imothy Kibodeaux insists he is no hero.

"The real heroes are the rescue workers and the people who died that day. I was just doing what I was trained to do," said the then-30 year-old Woodbridge, CT college student with a shrug. A traumatic brain injury forced him to retire from the U.S Navy three years before 9/11. But that didn't stop him from seeking a way to help.

Kibodeaux was one of the Navy's elite Sea, Air, Land (SEAL) commandos for six years before a fluke pool accident relegated him to early retirement. Becoming a SEAL puts a man through what some considered the toughest military training in the world. Humility is drummed into the commandos.

Even though Kibodeaux had to retire, the Navy lists him as a reservist. That's how the New York State Police came to call upon him on September 11th. They wanted to make use of his underwater search expertise to find any incendiary explosives that might be planted on piers or underwater stanchions surrounding the island of Manhattan.

"They weren't sure what the extent of terrorist activity was at that point and there were very few trained divers who could do the job," he said. "They initially were going to bring two warships into the area, and they needed someone to sweep the piers, the docks, any possible structure that an explosive could be attached to.

"I was more than happy to lend a hand if I could," he said. I am not a person who wants to sit around at home and just send money in as a donation. I am a hands-on person."

Kibodeaux's SEAL training served him as soon he hit New York waters. Though the water was no more than 35 feet deep, visibility was poor. Under the water, it was black as night. He used an underwater flashlight. He found he was one of the few who knew what to look for.

"You can't blame them," he said of the other divers. "Their experience had really been looking for bodies, or guns and weapons in those waters," he said. "Primarily what we were looking for was something as large as a 55-gallon steel drum or a refrigerator. Something that would be large enough to rip through a three-foot thick wall of a warship or aircraft carrier."

Fortunately, he found nothing after diving for five days. That reinforced his hunch that the terrorists did not plan as thoroughly as they could have.

"I didn't think we would find anything. It just didn't appear to be that intricate of an attack," he said.

But being in Manhattan right after the attack gave him the same sense of foreboding he had doing other dangerous missions for the military.

"I had the opportunity one time to rescue a downed helicopter pilot, but I can't tell you where," he explained. "There were some friendlies who had secured the area, but we did not know that at the time. I don't know if I was actually worried, but there is a feeling—a feeling like, you just don't know what to expect. I had that same feeling walking around down there. I thought, 'Jeez, I could be walking around down here and anything could explode.' And this could be going on in all our major metropolitan areas."

Even with the experiences he has had, Kibodeaux said he was shocked to see the extent of the devastation in Manhattan.

"I've seen this stuff happen everywhere else but here. If you'd asked me if it could have ever happened here, I would have told you it was the furthest thing from my mind. Not in a million years."

# ON THE WINGS OF PEACE

"I WILL WRITE PEACE on your wings and you will fly all over the world." So wrote Sadako Sasaki over 60 years ago. She was 2 years old when the atom bomb was dropped on Hiroshima on Aug. 6, 1945.

Sadako survived the blast and grew into an athletic child. At age 11, she was practicing for a big race, when she suddenly became dizzy and collapsed. Physicians diagnosed her with leukemia. The probable cause: exposure to the fallout from the atom bomb.

Sadako wanted desperately to live. She knew of a Japanese legend that said that if a person folds 1,000 paper cranes, her wish will come true. In Japan, cranes have long been a symbol of hope. So Sadako began making cranes out of paper, using the ancient Japanese art of origami. According to some accounts, she completed 644 before she died. Others say she completed 1,000.

Either way, her wish was not granted. Sadako Sasaki died on Oct. 25, 1955 at the age of 12. Her classmates continued to fold paper cranes in her memory. Today, people all over the world fold paper cranes and send them to Sadako's monument in Hiroshima. Inscribed at the bottom is her dying wish for the world she left behind: "This is our cry, this is our prayer, peace in the world." Since then, the paper crane has come to be a symbol of peace, of a world where children everywhere are safe and where people live in harmony.

Sadako's stories inspired several peace initiatives, including one called the Sadako Project. Students who belong to the Asian Pacific Student Program at the University of California, Riverside, were apparently familiar with Sadako and the legend surrounding the cranes. They decided to fold one paper crane for each victim of the terrorist attacks. Then they strung them together to create a display, symbolizing their dream for peace for each and every one.

A Massachusetts teacher had a similar idea. Sarah Nixon of Medfield, MA, asked her students at Dale Elementary School to create thousands of paper cranes. She was inspired by the World Peace Project for Children, a Puget Sound, WA, organization that adopted the paper crane as its symbol for world peace.

Nixon is a marathon runner. She told students she would hand deliver the cranes to New York during the New York City Marathon on Nov. 4. Nixon has run to help raise money for good causes before, but she told her students that this time, she was running for peace. The cranes would be her symbol.

Her students did not let her down. They folded 8,000 cranes in time for her run. Before Nixon left for New York, she packed 5,000 of the cranes in hockey bags, so she could carry them with her on the train. She had another 10,000 shipped directly to the hotel where she would be staying. When she got to New York, she strung them all together in a garland. She brought the garland out so she could have pictures taken with it. She had one taken with a police officer, after she explained how much the children appreciated the hard work of the New York City police department on September 11th.

When she got together with the other runners, she draped the garland of cranes around her neck.

"There was a woman from Japan wearing a kimono over her running clothes," Nixon said. "She came up smiling to me when she saw the cranes. Because I was competing in this marathon, I could not run the 26 miles with a whole garland of cranes, but I did pin about six to my running clothes that accompanied me along the course."

Nixon said she found the last two miles of the race so difficult she felt like walking the rest of the way, "but the spirit of Sadako and the children who made the 8,000 cranes gave me the courage and determination to keep on running and finish the race."

Nixon clocked in at two hours and 56 minutes, making her the third person to finish from New England and the 51st female to cross the finish line. She said it was an honor to run the marathon "as the messenger of all the children in the world who fold cranes."

Before she left New York, she brought the cranes to city librarians who assured her that they would distribute them equally to the city's 82 branches. The 2,000 paper cranes Nixon left behind in Medfield are now on display at the town's library.

"I will write peace on your wings and you will fly all over the world," said Sadako so many years ago. She was right. In the autumn of 2001, the cranes took flight again.

# THE RIGHT PLACE AT THE RIGHT TIME

IT WAS MORE THAN being in the right place at the right time. It was one of those once-in-a lifetime moments when fate taps you on the shoulder and says, NOW.

Paul Amico acted purely on instinct. Amico was working at the dock in Weehawken, NJ, directly across the Hudson River from the World Trade Center. When he saw the smoke rising from the Twin Towers, he knew something was drastically wrong. He didn't waste time. He didn't consult his boss or wait for someone to tell him what to do. Instead, the NY Waterway construction supervisor took matters into his own hands. He grabbed a marine two-way radio and hopped a ferry heading toward lower Manhattan. Like everyone else that fateful morning, he did not know the extent and magnitude of the destruction. But it was shaping up as a disaster, and he knew people would need a way to get off the island of Manhattan.

Time proved him right. The collapse of the first tower left a mountain of debris on the World Financial Center dock, the main loading barge for the New York Waterway. It blocked access to the dock, creating yet another obstruction for fleeing financial-district workers. Amico used his two-way radio to warn incoming ferries of the problem, then took it upon himself to reroute them to a seawall at Battery Park, just a few hundred yards away. But when gas leaks created a dangerous situation near the seawall, he redirected the ferries to Pier 24 farther up the coast, which was still within walking distance for the evacuees.

How did Amico know what to do? His job was to build docks. He wasn't trained in directing ferries or in supervising a mass evacuation. But life had prepared him well. Amico was a kayaker. For the past three years, he had run kayaking trips for a recreational club located on that pier, so he knew the Hudson surrounding Pier 24. He knew that it was nine feet deep, just enough to allow the ferries to move in and out without getting stuck.

"I know the water," he said. "I knew they [evacuees] would need help. It freed up managers to go elsewhere."

But there were still challenges. Even though he knew the rec. club dock could handle the ferry traffic, getting the fleeing masses to the dock was a problem. A chain-link fence blocked their way to the incoming ferries. Luckily, Amico was a member of the recreational club, and he had a key to the boathouse in his pocket. In the boathouse was an acetylene torch. Amico used it to cut an opening in the fence large enough for people to pass.

For the next two and a half hours, the NY Waterways ferried people— most of them injured, all of them frightened and dazed— across the Hudson River to Jersey City. Some 48,000 people found their way out of Manhattan that way.

Amico was one of many—and there were many in Washington, in the air and in Manhattan—who felt the prompting of fate on September 11th and had the courage and the presence of mind to act.

# CHEFS WITH SPIRIT

AFTER PEOPLE HEARD about the terrific work the New York rescue crew was doing, everyone wanted to feed them. Donations came from restaurants, private citizens and churches groups throughout New York and across the country. Getting food wasn't a problem. Getting it to the rescuers was. The obstacles: horrible traffic and tight security checkpoints. In the first weeks after September 11th, police were stopping vans and trucks so they could check their contents.

"It was an absolute nightmare," said Don Pintabona, executive chef of Tribeca Grill, a chic restaurant co-owned by Robert DeNiro. "We had food donated from every part of America, but it wasn't getting downtown."

The grill is just 11 blocks north of Ground Zero. It became inaccessible to its regular clientele after police cordoned off the surrounding neighborhoods. So Pintabona decided to use the kitchen to cook for the rescue workers. Plenty of New York chefs were eager to help. But they had a problem to solve first.

Then a fellow chef cracked a joke about shipping the food to the workers. Why not? After all, Pintabona thought, Manhattan is an island. "Why's everyone trying to go down by road?"

He used his contacts to speak to the folks at Spirit Cruises, a company that owns the dinner-cruise vessels that sail the Hudson. They were able to work out an arrangement. Three days after the attacks, Pintabona and crew were ready to serve on board a 192-foot boat tied up at a marina in Battery Park City—about eight blocks from Ground Zero. They named the operation "Chefs with Spirit." The speed with which the operation came together was unbelievable, said Pintabona.

The floating restaurant, which seats 100, served 3000 to 7,000 meals a day during that time. Even in New York, that's impressive.

Since the operation began, donations and volunteer chefs kept it going. They stuck to comfort foods, but being the creative chefs that they were, they couldn't help giving the basics a little extra flair.

Rescue workers were extremely grateful. They weren't shy about letting the chefs know.

"A guy came up to me and said, 'Look, I gotta tell you, this is the best meal I've ever had in my life, and I've never been on a boat,'" recalled Pintabona with a laugh. Maybe that's not the kind of reviews a New York chef could build a reputation on, but it makes the hot hours in the kitchen even more gratifying.

Pintabona eventually turned the operation over to the Red Cross.

But Nino Vendome, owner of Nino's Restaurant at 431 Canal Street, kept his restaurant open to give rescue workers free food for as long as donations kept coming in and the need remained. "As long as they're in the rubble, we're in the rubble," he'd said.

With the help of volunteers, such as Tavern on the Green chef Gary Coyle, Vendome kept the restaurant open 24 hours a day for months after the attacks. The place became a home away from home for the rescue workers, who knew they could come there for a free hot meal. And come they did—local police officers, state troopers, national guardsmen, demolition experts, firefighters and folks in the construction trade.

Although the restaurant served 150 meals a day on a typical day before 9/11, it dished out close to 6,000 meals a day since Sept. 13th through the cleanup effort. That's a lot of tomato sauce. Fortunately, others contributed to help offset the costs, but Vendome foot the bill for everything that donations don't cover. By October, Nino had spent a million dollars of his own money covering the shortfall.

Vendome, whose family emigrated from Italy in 1955 with $40 and four suitcases, said he felt compelled to do something concrete to show appreciation for the rescue workers.

"We do what we know how to do," said Vendome, with a laugh. "We take care of people."

# A LEVEL PLAYING FIELD

MANHATTAN IS HOME to hundreds of public relations firms, all of them in heated competition for the same lucrative accounts. It is not a field that promotes camaraderie among fellow industry members.

But something close to a miracle happened after September 11th. The industry came together in a spirit of service to help non-profit service organizations like the American Red Cross handle the flood of media calls from around the world. Who knew better how to handle reporters, funnel requests and get out information swiftly and accurately than New York's PR community?

A human resources manager for Manhattan-based Cohn & Wolfe Healthcare, a global public relations firm representing mostly pharmaceutical companies, worked out a way with the American Red Cross in which peer professionals could help. "We were just one company that jumped in," said Caren Wagner, a media specialist for Cohn & Wolfe. "After working our usual hours, we then worked the graveyard shift for eight to 12 hours overnight, fielding media calls, writing media alerts with updated information, doing anything we could."

Also heeding the call was Stanton Crenshaw Communications, which has offices in Manhattan and Southern California'.

"It was a very level playing field and it was amazing," said Peter Engel, an account supervisor for the mid-sized public relations firm. "At the end of the day after pulling my shift at the Red Cross, I was amazed when I found out who I was working next to. A lot of them had some pretty hefty responsibilities at their firms. Yet there was no time during the day that they alluded to who they were or what they did. They were just there to help."

What the experience gave the volunteers was a way to help.

"So many were involved," said Wagner. "What's amazing is that through such a tragedy, people were smiling and happy being together and working." She said that hundreds of public relations specialists donated their time during the first few days following the attacks. Although it was a challenge to keep the operation flowing smoothly and orderly, they did it.

It helped many of them get through the period. "We were not functioning that week, and we really didn't function for several weeks after that," said Engel. "Our industry has taken a bit of drubbing, but we proved our value there and then," he added.

Stanton Crenshaw, like other public relations firms, encouraged its clients to find their own unique way to serve.

"One of our clients, Starbucks, served 424,000 cups of coffee at Ground Zero and the Pier 94 family assistance center. Six of our staff members volunteered their time to just serve coffee. Starbucks has a whole outreach program," he said.

Wagner enjoyed helping so much she continued to volunteer her free time around the city to assist survivors and rescue workers.

"I think a bunch of us felt helpless when it all happened, especially when it became clear that the people most needed were medical professionals," said Wagner. "I wished then that I were a doctor. But I was only in public relations. When this opportunity happened, it was great. I had something to offer. And it was such a rewarding experience."

But she and the others wished they could have done more.

"Compared to cops and firemen, relief and rescue workers who were doing a much more important job, [what we did] doesn't feel like it was adequate," she said. "What happened is so enormous."

## AMERICA'S TEENS PITCH IN

LITTLE AIDIN FONTANA saluted the 1,000 firefighters at ·his dad's funeral as he sat in the black limousine next to his mother,· Marian. His father's helmet was on his lap. But the coffin was empty. Aidin's father, David, a firefighter from Squad No. 1 in Park Slope, Brooklyn, was still listed as missing. His body had not been found. That made his mother uneasy.

"It wasn't a funeral for me," she said. "I didn't have a body. I don't feel closure and maybe I never will."

Aidin's school friends put together a book for him, tucking in stories about him and his hero father. Others brought him presents and letters to cheer him up. He loves his father and will never forget his father's love for him. It's for children like Aidin Fontana that the youth of America unite.

Compelled by the same need to "do something" that spurred adults into action, a small group of teenagers in Pennsylvania and Connecticut started High Schools for Heroes. The name stems from the group's belief that "every person who died—whether on the ground, in a plane or in an office building—was a true American hero." Their mission: to get high school students across the country involved in a massive campaign to raise money for the children who lost their parents as a result of the terrorists attacks.

Organizers challenged participating schools to complete their fundraisers by Dec. 1, 2001. The group promised that 100 percent of the money raised would be earmarked for children and given to The September 11th Fund, a national fund backed by the United Way. None of the money would be used for administrative costs.

Hundreds of schools—from Gig Harbor, WA, to Miami—responded. In short order, the original organizers put up a web site to spread the word. By Sept. 24, they managed to get the U.S. Department of Education to agree to add a link on its web site to assist schools in handling the crisis. The group also signed on a host of corporate sponsors, including the Coca-Cola Company.

The group's motto is, "One person can't do everything, but everybody can do something."

The initiative seems to have done as much for the teens as for the children they're trying to help. Teens, who often feel disenfranchised and at odds with society, discovered how good it feels to make a contribution.

Participating schools came up with a variety of fundraising ideas, some traditional, some novel.

The students at the Agnes Irwin School in Rosemont, PA had a bake sale. Everything was moderately priced-between a dime and 50 cents per snack-and it was common for customers to overpay. One person paid $50 for a single fudge brownie.

Students at Sachem High School in Lake Ronkonkoma, NY, established a Sachem Emergency Relief Team to collect supplies for the rescue workers, establish trust funds for Sachem district children who had lost a parent in the attacks and raise funds for relevant charities. Because of Lake Ronkonkoma's proximity to Manhattan, many in the community were directly affected by the terrorist attacks.

The industrious teens delivered over two tons of supplies to rescue workers in the first month of their initiative. They also raised $15,000 toward their other two goals. One successful fundraiser was their "Oldies for America" concert. They targeted the right generation: people old enough to have money to give.

In Philadelphia, students from Northeast High School took a multi-prong approach. The Student Senate began selling ribbons for victim's relief immediately after September 11th. Art classes set to work creating six large boards with messages of hope for three fire houses and three high schools located close to Ground Zero. The students also put together a gala event for March 2002, inviting the firefighters and police officers who spearheaded the rescue efforts, and their families, for a fun-filled day in Philadelphia. Among the activities: a celebrity-studded dinner, with students serving as waiters and waitresses, and a sightseeing tour the next day.

Teenagers at Boiling Springs High School in South Carolina raised money for victim relief. They sold cutouts of the Capitol, World Globes and Bulldog Heads, their mascot. They raffled off the principal's parking space. For a buck, they sold students the "privilege" of wearing a hat to school. They also charged kids to park in the school lot and asked parents and other members of the community for cash donations.

The students raised $15,233.50 on their own, then shrewdly sought corporate matching funds. Bi-Lo Inc. of Mauldin, SC said, 'Yes,' bringing the grand total to $30,467.

These were just teenagers but they gave their all, including their free time in the evenings and on weekends. In the currency of teenagers, that's a lot. Yet they felt the power in coming together to make a difference.

## 84 AND TIRELESS TO THE END

OVER A HALF A CENTURY AGO, when the US entered World War II, Anthony Bai signed up for the military the day the draft took effect. After the war, he devoted most of his life to helping wounded veterans, like himself, who were lucky to still be alive, but carried the wounds that only war can administer. He loved America so much that he saved money so his sister—who had been left behind in war-torn Poland—could come live here, too.

When Bai's wife Vickie died several years ago, his family worried that he might not last much longer himself. Bai had diabetes and had undergone multiple bypass surgery just a few years before his wife's death. His heart wasn't strong and he had lost the love of his life. But Bai was a survivor.

After his wife died, Bai moved to Washington to be closer to his two daughters. He threw himself back into life with a relish that commanded their admiration. Never one to let the grass grow under his feet, he took computer classes, bought a new condo and went on.

When the terrorists hatched their ghastly plan, it spurred veterans like Anthony Bai to action. It never occurred to Bai that he was 84. He still had the spunk of an 18-year-old. So, over the protests of his daughters, Bai struck out for the Pentagon.

He was promptly, although politely, turned away. Undaunted, he went to the Salvation Army; an organization he knew would welcome an old-time vet like himself. On Sept. 16, he went to work sorting and repackaging medical supplies. While it wasn't exactly the type of work he'd envisioned—he was surprised that others thought him too old and frail to pull bodies from the rubble—he did his duty with a soldier's pride.

At the end of the long, tedious day, Bai felt fulfilled but exhausted. He enjoyed the feeling that came with making himself useful—so much so that he ignored his exhaustion and signed up for another day. After a warm meal with one of his children, he set off for home. He told his daughter he would call when he got there, to ease her mind.

The call never came.

Anthony Bai died of a heart attack that night. The old soldier had spent his last day, and the last of his energy, serving his country.

## SERVING GOD AMIDST THE RUBBLE

THE DAY WAS HOT and the air still thick with the putrid, pungent smell that hung in lower Manhattan like the haze in August. The first thing that Beth Ralston noticed when she arrived to do volunteer work at Seaman's Institute, a relief site set up near Ground Zero, was a debris-covered St. Paul's Cemetery. "You couldn't see the gravestones. It was absolutely strewn with papers, covered with what must have been piles and piles of correspondence from people's offices." Scattered among the debris were the skeletons of people whose flesh had disintegrated from the fiery temperatures inside the towers.

"It was indescribable. It was utterly devastating," she said, adding that nothing, even the television broadcasts, had prepared her for what she saw. Raltson, executive assistant to the rector of St. Bartholomew's Episcopal Church, took charge of coordinating the church's volunteer efforts.

In the wake of the disaster, the General Theological Episcopal Seminary in New York had been asked to coordinate round-the-clock relief shifts at the church, which is located off of Peck's Slip on South Street close to the financial district. St. Bart's was one of many churches to heed the call.

"They asked us to provide enough volunteers for two 24-hour shifts," she said. "We decided to send eight people for four hours at a time. They needed food donations as well, stuff you could eat right away, like hamburgers, hot dogs—no canned foods. They needed clothing, boots, socks, dog food, flashlights, batteries. All kinds of stuff that they could eat and go, or grab and take away."

Would the congregation come through? At first, Ralston wasn't sure. The well-heeled congregants at St. Bart had never been asked to give so much of their time before. The call for volunteers went out on a Thursday at the evening Eucharist service. When Ralston returned to her office on Saturday morning and checked her voice mail and e-mail, she was overwhelmed.

"There were 85 messages. That's just in a day and a half." She stopped counting the emails that jammed her mailbox. "People were desperately seeking to help in some way."

The response was so overwhelming that Ralston made sure that those who volunteered knew exactly what was expected of them. "The things that we were instructed to tell people were pretty sobering. I told them that they could be cooking or doing cleanup at Seaman's

Institute or going down to Ground Zero and working in the hole, which was pretty intense."

But no one said, 'No.' Overall, the church sent 112 volunteers to work those two days. They could have covered many more shifts, if needed. "One of the unbelievable things to me was that I was getting calls from housewives with children, who said they would be happy to work the midnight to 4 a.m. shift and then go back home to take care of their families."

Ralston joined the volunteers close to Ground Zero and was glad she did. Despite the overwhelming rush of sadness she felt, she donned an apron and began to focus on the task at hand.

"The overwhelming desire was to help the rescue workers to do their job Even though I was utterly devastated, I was there to help these people and show my support. And the really strange thing was, they were so incredibly thankful that the volunteers were there. They were kind, polite and encouraging. Here I'm just flipping hamburgers and they're thanking me! It was hot and I think a smile and a few nice words went a long way before they had to go back to work."

Ralston keep on volunteering, doing what she could long afterwards. Weeks after the relief center at Seaman's shut down, the calls kept coming from congregation members and nearby churches looking to send volunteers. People really wanted to help. She remembers working alongside a gentleman in an expensive business suit.

"He had taken the day off and went down there to help. He was very quiet most of the time," she said. "Not really talking, just working. And he finally turned to me and said, 'You know what? I have raised a lot of money for charity events over the years and have always considered myself a philanthropist. But this is the most important thing I have ever done in my life.' I think that was the feeling of everyone down there."

## BOULEY'S ALL-NIGHT KITCHEN

BOULEY BAKERY, on West Broadway in Manhattan's TriBeCa neighborhood, isn't a bakery, exactly. It's the kind of place that serves up dishes like organic baby lamb with eggplant moussaka and skate steamed with fresh chamomile. Its food rated 27 out of a possible 30 in Zagat's. One of its chefs, Galen Zamarra, was named a rising-star chef in the age-30-and-under category in the James Beard Foundation award ceremony.

Clearly, it doesn't need any help in the public relations category.

But that didn't stop owner David Bouley from turning his upscale eatery into a cafeteria for rescue workers at Ground Zero, He was among hundreds in the restaurant industry who pitched in to provide nourishing food for those on the front lines of hell.

Restaurants like Bouley Bakery took in volunteers so they could keep the kitchen running virtually all night. With the help of over 700 volunteers, Bouley was turning out 34,000 meals per day. The volunteers were delighted to be able to give their time to such a worthy undertaking.

"It is hard to describe the joy in feeling that you're helping, that you're engaged in such a worthy cause," Philip Weiss, one of the many Bouley volunteers, wrote in *The New York Observer*. "The amount of food going in and out was staggering: boxes and boxes of cucumbers, buckets of squash, aquarium-sized bins full of rice, 150-pound Styrofoam fish boxes piled on the sidewalk."

The operation went through several thousand pounds each day of salmon, chicken, beef and assorted donations, like the pig from a Vermont farm.

Bouley, a renowned chef, supervised the massive effort, making sure that the salmon with mustard sauce was cooked to his exacting standards. "It wasn't to be baked, but seared and fried, and pink inside, " wrote Weiss.

Apparently, Bouley's strictness paid off. During that time, Tom Zagat, known for his restaurant guide, visited Bouley Bakery. Chef Bouley handed him a plate of the meal du jour: pork mixed with potatoes, parsnip and celery, and asked for a rating from 1 to 30.

"Well, it would definitely get a VI for Very Inexpensive," Zagat joked. Then he got serious. "I would say the food rating comes close to a 28, because it exceeded my expectations," said Zagat. "And I would give it a 32 for generosity." Many other restaurateurs and caterers were just as generous. Starbucks, for instance, served half a million cups of free coffee the first month after the attacks, thanks to volunteers who made cup after cup of cappuccino and espresso for eight to 12 hours at a clip. On the one-month anniversary of the attacks, more than 300 restaurants in New York City and hundreds of others elsewhere donated at least 10 percent of the evening's proceeds to Windows of Hope, an organization created to helping families of victims, especially food-service workers. They did this despite the fact that Manhattan restaurants—hurting because of a fall-off in tourism—could ill-afford to give away profits.

# KEEP PEDALING

NITHY SEVANTHINATHAN is an optimist and an absolute original. The Malaysian immigrant came to the United States to study at Minnesota State University over a decade ago and has been here ever since. When he's not traveling—which is often—he works as assistant director of the university's International Student office.

But his real passion is helping out in the aftermath of a crisis. "I have worked in floods, earthquakes and other natural disasters, doing whatever people need, whatever I can do to help," he said. So, naturally, he headed to New York after September 11th. He waited a reasonable two weeks, then called the Red Cross beforehand to see where he was needed most. The organization assigned him to the family crisis center on Pier 94.

Sevanthinathan was needed there because of his translation skills. Not only is he conversant in the dialects of his native Malaysia, including Bahasa Malaysia and Tamil; he's also able to speak Spanish and Chinese Hokkien. He used his skill to help family members who were missing loved ones, most of whom worked in maintenance and food-service jobs at the World Trade Center. He also made himself available for more menial jobs.

"I am very flexible. I told them I would pick up garbage, or clean up bathrooms," he said. "I didn't care. I'm sure they were surprised to see a Minnesotan and a Malaysian by birth assisting them, but this happened to all of us. Not just New Yorkers."

Sevanthinathan found enough to do to keep himself busy during the day, but he was too restless at night to sleep much. He struggled with the question of why the terrorists had done this.

"I could not understand how a person could have that kind of evil mentality," he said. "I was really shocked and I think we need to understand why this happened. Why do they hate America so much?"

For Sevanthinathan, with his childlike innocence, found the answers were particularly hard to fathom. This is a man who considered it his mission to travel the world by bicycle and touch hearts wherever he went. In one decade, he traveled to 70 countries on four continents, taking nothing but his bike, backpack and the money he earned from his job.

"Every expedition I do, I meet people, I meet children for I am trying to learn from them," he said. "I rely on the concept of sharing, which I truly believe in. I share a lot. My goal is that when I finally pedal back home, I only have in my possession the clothes I am wearing—a T-shirt and shorts. I give everything else away. I have extra money with me, and I give it to the children."

His travels have taken him from rural Oklahoma to the remote corners of Argentina. "I bicycle through towns, talk to people and just knock on doors and ask if I can spend the night. No one has said 'No.'"

During his extraordinary travels, the humanitarian cyclist has found that people across the world share several fundamental beliefs. These have shaped his worldview.

"I believe that every single human in his or her heart wants peace," he said. What happened on September 11th "went against everything that I have seen to be true across this world. Everyone is unique, every culture has its own gifts, but people are basically the same. This was just so shocking.

"Perhaps the one thing to come out of this is that tragedy brings the best out of us," he continued, adding that in a strange way, it was heavenly volunteering at Pier 94. "We all had the same goal. And we saw how much we can do when we unite. It was like paradise."

Sevanthinathan resolved to keep that spirit of unity alive as he went about his business each day.

"For instance, when I see a police officer today, I will reach out to him and ask how he is doing. And I thank him. I want him to know that I will share his struggle along the way."

The credo he lives by is this: "Life is no straight and easy corridor along which we travel free and unhampered, but a maze of passages, through which we must seek our way, lost and confused, now and again checked in a blind alley," he said. "But always, if we have faith, a door will open for us. Not perhaps one that we ourselves would ever have thought of, but one that will ultimately prove good for us."

# LEADERS WORTH NOTING

## REMEMBERING NEW YORK'S FIVE-STAR FIRE CHIEF

The last time his men saw him, Peter Ganci, New York City fire chief, was doing the job he loved. The universally loved and highest-ranking official in the city's fire department was working side by side with his men at the World Trade Center. He survived the first collapse, but instead of moving back out of harm's way, he went toward the collapse to supervise rescues.

"Right from the beginning, the department was led by its five-star hero, Peter Ganci," Acting Chief Dan Nigro said in his eulogy. "The look he had on his face was . . . like Mel Gibson in *Braveheart*. He was a warrior."

Just moments before, Ganci had been with the mayor in a makeshift command post. As the mayor was leaving to go to the police command center a few blocks away, he turned to Ganci and said, "God Bless you." Ganci returned the blessing. "Thank you and God bless you."

"I thought I would see him later," Giuliani sadly remembered.

In his homily, the Rev. John Delendick recalled Ganci, 54, as someone who "preferred to be one of the guys." He was the type who lead by example. Rev. Delendick, who was on the scene that day in his role as a fire department chaplain, recalled seeing Ganci "right in front, as he always is, and in control. He had this look of defiance on his face. It was as if he was looking at the fire, saying, 'I'm going to get you,'" Delendick said.

But as the danger intensified, Ganci was ordered to move the fire command post north out of the north tower, which he did, and safely away from the soon-to-be-imploding buildings.

Then he went "south to check on the other command post. His

decision saved so many lives," Delendick said.

Ganci had been a firefighter for 33 years, and a highly decorated one at that. A family friend inspired his career choice. "Of all my parents' friends, the only one happy going to work was a member of 120 Truck. I was only 16 then, but that is when I decided I wanted to be a fireman," he once said.

As department chief, Ganci was responsible for both fire and EMS operations, training and fire Prevention. He was also required to represent uniformed members of the NYFD at ceremonial functions.

Making the transition to top dog had its downside. The deep bonds between firefighters are forged at the firehouse. That's where the action is. Few firefighters relish the idea of working out of the department's headquarters. But even though Ganci dearly loved being where the action is, he viewed his assignment at headquarters as a way of "giving back to the fire department," and an opportunity to make things better for the firefighters coming after us."

Still, the job was not without its frustrations. He once complained that he spent "an excessive amount of time trying to resolve one conflict or another. Most of the issues I face daily are problems of some sort. It doesn't leave much time to acknowledge the good our guys do every day." He said that one of the most difficult aspects of his job was "striking a balance between an obligation to the public and our members. I continually strive to do the right thing by both."

Over 4,000 attended Ganci's funeral. While the words of "Danny Boy" drifted over the crowd, Ganci was laid to rest in a flag-draped coffin. His youngest son, Christopher, held his father's white helmet and sobbed as he remembered his dad. "Whether you were a foreign dignitary or a man in the street, he made you feel important," he said. "I love you and am so happy to be your son."

Ganci's brother, Daniel, a colonel in the reserves heading the 1179th Deployment Support Battalion, struggled with the death of his older brother. But he was not surprised. When he heard of the collapse, no one had to tell him that his brother was dead. "He had to be there," he said. "He was my hero all the time. He was one hell of a man, the consummate firefighter."

Ganci had always wanted to be remembered "as a good fireman and a good chief," he had said. He was all that and more.

# ARLINGTON'S VISIONARY FIRE CHIEF

WHEN AMERICAN AIRLINES Flight 77 plowed into the side of the Pentagon on September 11th, igniting it and thickening the air with black fumes from the jet fuel, Arlington Fire Chief Edward Plaugher had the presence of mind to find the best vantage point from which to supervise the firefighting and rescue efforts. He knew Assistant Fire Chief James Schwartz was doing an excellent job handling things on the ground, so he raced to a U.S. Park Helicopter. He ducked under its whirling blades, pointed to the words "Fire Chief" emblazoned on his helmet, then stuck his finger up in the air. The pilot obliged him.

Surveying the scene from the chopper, directly above the Pentagon, Plaugher radioed his assistant fire chief to stay the course. He warned him that more of the building might collapse. They continued to direct hundreds of firefighters and paramedics at the site.

"It was a brilliant move on his part," said Schwartz. "What he recognized was that there was need for somebody to be looking at all the pieces. From where I was standing, while it was awesome in its scope, you couldn't see the whole thing."

But it wasn't so much what Plaugher did at the scene that catapulted him from dedicated fire chief to national hero. It was the actions he had taken over many years to help the Arlington, VA/Washington, DC, metropolitan area prepare for such an event.

Plaugher had told any official who would listen that the region was not sufficiently prepared to handle a terrorist attack. Back in 1995, he had gone before the Washington Council of Governments to suggest that it seek help from the federal government. He told them he had analyzed the likely response to a chemical or biological attack, and things "looked pretty bleak." He suggested solutions.

Later that year, spurred by Plaugher, Congress created the Metropolitan Medical Response Service. The MMRS was to be established in major cities around the country and supply teams of firefighters and paramedics trained to handle the aftermath of terrorist attacks, including chemical warfare.

The idea was that the MMRS would do it more efficiently and with fewer casualties. Teams would be responsible for ensuring the safety of those on the scene. They would also provide emergency medical services, mental health services, hygienic handling of the dead, decontamination of victims and the deployment of patients to regional health-care facilities. They would understand all the nuances of chemical warfare. They would know how to triage patients and how to handle the ongoing crisis.

Plaugher, a public servant for 34 years, had already anticipated the next wave of urban disasters. And while banging the drum loudly didn't made him the most popular guy in town, September 11th did prove him right. The result of his foresight was evident that day at the Pentagon. No rescue worker was killed in the line of duty that day.

"From the day he came in, he always had a broad approach," said Mike Staples, president of the Arlington Professional Firefighters and Paramedics Association. "He thinks outside the box. Mass casualty. Terrorism. There were skeptics."

But maybe not so many now.

# IN PAIN, YET VERY MUCH IN CONTROL

FOR NEW YORK CITY Fire Commissioner Thomas Von Essen, September 11th began with the unforgettable sight of people falling from the towering infernos, and hearing the macabre, deafening thud as they hit the pavement. It got worse as it wore on: his four top aides were killed right near him. He and Mayor Rudy Giuliani narrowly escaped their own deaths when the second tower collapsed. But his grief had to be put aside, because the commissioner had a job to do. It was a job that would get tougher as the days wore on.

He had to make hard decisions fast. On that day, he assembled as many of the senior chiefs and battalions as he could at Ground Zero. He told them their priority was to "rescue as many as you can." To do so, "we took enormous risks early on," he said. He did not know the extent of the danger, or that the smoldering fires would continue for weeks after the collapse. After he ushered in the rescue efforts, he brought in heavy equipment to help drag out the large pieces of melted, twisted steel.

Photos of him throughout the days following the disaster showed two seemingly different men: a poker-faced leader standing next to the mayor at media press conferences, and a man on the verge of emotional collapse, fighting back tears. During one of the many memorials for one of his "guys" the camera captured him with his head in his hands, wracked with grief. "There are 341 firefighters and two EMTs but they are all individuals," he said. "You go to the service, and you're looking at the guy's son and daughter . . .To see that little kid just breaks your heart."

Among those killed were friends, top chiefs, veteran elite rescuers and entire companies. In his 20 years as a firefighter in New York's tough South Bronx, the 55-year-old firefighter, once head of the fire union, thought he had seen it all. But as the death toll for firefighters kept climbing, the shock of losing so many in one day leveled him. "If a broken heart can kill you, I could die any minute," he told a reporter.

To make matters even worse, he found himself facing the excruciating task of replacing the firefighters he had known and loved. He knew that if he didn't, he'd leave the New York Fire Department precariously understaffed.

But when to do it? He agonized over that question, knowing the ceremony to promote the new firefighters would be incredibly painful for the victims' families. Still, he knew he needed to take control. He told those gathered at the ceremony to promote 168 members to officer rank, "We are shaken, but we are not defeated. We stare adversity in the eye, and we push on."

Von Essen once again showed his stony composure at that ceremony. At times, the look in his blue eyes can be steely and decisive. Perhaps he was drawing on his philosophy that leaders do what they have to do and put personal issues aside. "I told anybody who's got a problem to suck it up and move on," he said.

But moving on has been extraordinarily hard for someone who considers himself responsible for the welfare of every one of the 11,000 men and women in the New York Fire Department. He feels so strongly about them that he'd risk his life to save theirs.

"It seems like I've been fighting with these guys for 15 years, and I love them," he said. "I absolutely love them."

Even as he has made the effort to rebuild the department during a time of unprecedented grief, he has tried to take stock of himself. "I don't think I've really focused in yet on the magnitude of the tragedy," said Von Essen. "I don't know how I'll come out of this emotionally. I don't know if it will ever be over for me."

## PUTTING SAFETY FIRST

A PHOTOGRAPH IN Police Commissioner Bernard Kerik's office shows him on the Brooklyn Bridge, standing next to James Vigiano, a detective in the Emergency Service Unit. The Twin Towers loom behind them. They are both smiling. It was taken just a few months before September 11th.

"He was a good cop," said Kerik. "I had singled him out and given him second grade," he remembered, blinking back a tear. Vigiano was among the 23 cops whose bodies were buried in the mountains of rubble on September 11th. His brother, John Vigiano II, a firefighter with Ladder 132, met a similar fate. They left their father, a battalion chief, to sift through the rubble with his own hands, trying to find them. They are the reason that Kerik keeps a carefully folded fire-singed flag, which used to hang over the World Trade Center, on his desk.

Kerik was a pivotal figure in the aftermath of the attack. He was a constant companion to the mayor, and like the mayor, almost lost his own life when the buildings collapsed. The tough decisions about closing the tunnels and bridges leading into Manhattan fell to him. So did the decision to institute checkpoints at those locations. For him, safety took precedence over all.

"I lived in Saudi Arabia and traveled in the Middle East. I understand the policing of foreign nations constantly under a blanket of terrorism," he shrugged. "It's unfortunate, but we have to live in a world of reality."

The largest criminal investigation in history hit a little closer to home for Kerik than for most. He had worked in Saudi Arabia, training security personnel and coordinating protection for the Saudi royal family and other heads of state. Kerik also married a Syrian. So he knows the price of safety. There's no place for thin skin. "If she or her family were stopped on an airplane during a routine check, they wouldn't object," he said, distinguishing between the terrorists and those who practice the Muslim faith. "Real Muslims are loving and caring people. Those are the people I knew when I lived over there. The people who did this hide behind the mask of religion."

The usually stoic Kerik was appointed the 40th police commissioner of New York by Mayor Rudy Giuliani on Aug. 21, 2000. As the leader of the largest municipal police department in the United States, Kerik oversees more than 41,000 officers. Prior to that, he was the commissioner of the Department of Correction.

Kerik began his career as a member of the United States Army's Military Police, serving for three years in Korea. In the 18th Airborne Corps, he trained Special Forces. He was a member of an all-Army martial arts team and is the recipient of a Medal of Valor. For all he's seen, however, he admits to being rattled by the events of September 11th. "When you talk to the families and see the guys looking for people they used to work with, it sinks in," he said. But then he adds with a dollop of hope, "As bad as this is, we can get through this."

# RUDY'S FINEST HOUR

*"There's nothing wrong with being afraid, but you don't give in to it."*
*—Rudy Giuliani*

SEPTEMBER 11TH, the morning of the primary elections, started just like every other workday for New York Mayor Rudolph Giuliani. He rose early in a friend s Upper East Side apartment and had a cup of coffee. He was in his office at City Hall, writing a note to his secretary, when American Airlines Flight 11—carrying 81 passengers, two pilots, nine flight attendants, and 13,900 gallons of jet fuel—slammed into the north tower of the World Trade Center. The explosion was so loud he could hear it in his office.

His counsel, Dennis Young, had passed along what little was known at the time: A plane had hit the World Trade Center. The first reports suggested that it was a twin engine or other small plane. They would later find out that it was a Boeing 757.

Giuliani, hoping to learn more at the scene, hopped into a SUV with his counsel and two police officers. He conferred with the police and fire commissioners by phone on the drive over. They tried to make sense of what had happened. He could see the flames lick the sky as his car got closer.

A few minutes later, at about 9:05 a.m., there was another earth-rattling boom. The mayor got the word on his car phone that a second plane had hit the south tower of the World Trade Center. The SUV sped the remaining two miles. By the time Giuliani and his officers got out of the car, the heat from the blaze was so intense it had caused glass to shatter from the upper-story windows. Shards were raining down from 100 stories above. The mayor watched, incredulous. He saw a man leap out of one of the upper-floor windows and plummet to his death. Giuliani had faced down cancer and prosecuted the mob, but he knew, as he surveyed what was going on around him, that he had never faced anything like this.

Top uniformed officials were already there, leading the evacuation from the north tower. Giuliani spoke with Fire Chief Peter Ganci at the scene, as well as with Father Mychal Judge, the fire departments much-loved chaplain. Both men would die shortly afterwards, in the performance of their duties. Giuliani's last words to Judge were: "Pray for us."

"I always do," Judge had replied with a grin.

The mayor left to set up what he thought would be a secure command post in an office just behind Seven World Trade Center. He tried to get someone from the White House on the line, but was told that it had been evacuated after the Pentagon attack. Vice President Cheney finally did call, but when Giuliani went to pick up the line it went dead. There was chaos all around. Around 10 a.m., the south tower collapsed in a ghostly column of ash and debris. Then the mayor's command post started to shake. He and his staff ran for their lives. They worked their way through a maze of stairs, first up, then down and finally through a corridor into another building.

"We were in a lot of danger," said Giuliani. "But at that time, there really wasn't time to think about it. I don't think I realized how bad it was," he added. "We were right behind Seven World Trade Center. And Seven World Trade Center absorbed the biggest hit from the fallen building and probably saved our lives."

They emerged into a landscape that resembled the aftermath of a nuclear blast.

"When that door opened, we all breathed a sigh of relief, although when we got into the lobby, I wasn't sure we were better off, because we looked outside and it looked like Armageddon," he said. "It was black and white, and there was no visibility at all."

A dazed Giuliani led his people to find another makeshift command post. Obviously, it had to be one with a working phone. As they walked and looked for an appropriate space, they continued to comfort people along the way. Finally, the mayor and his crew came to Engine Co. 24 on Houston Street, emptied when firefighters there responded to the first alarms. Giuliani used the fire station's phone and got confirmation from the White House about the attack on the Pentagon. He conferred about the best way to handle the current crisis, then readied himself to comfort the people of New York in a live broadcast interview.

In that first interview, a new Giuliani—calm, composed, compassionate—emerged.

"My heart goes out to the people," he said. "I've never seen anything like this. I was there from shortly after it happened and saw people jumping out of the World Trade Center. It's a horrible, horrible situation, and all that I can tell them is that every resource that we have is attempting to rescue as many people as possible. The end result is going to be some horrendous number of lives lost. I don't think we yet know, but right now we have to just focus on saving as many people as possible."

He maintained his composure throughout the day, even as the news kept getting worse. Ganci was killed just 15 minutes after Giuliani left him at the scene. Father Judge was also killed as he administered last rites to a fallen firefighter. Giuliani knew dozens of the 343 firefighters who lost their lives under the collapse. Hinting at his own grief, he would later answer questions about the death toll by saying the number was "more than any of us could bear."

At a press conference Giuliani held several hours after his first broadcast interview, he continued to extend his sympathy to affected families and to reassure them that the city would do its utmost to rescue everyone still trapped in the rubble.

"Today is obviously one of the most difficult days in the history of the city and the country," he said. "The tragedy that we're all undergoing right now is something that we've had nightmares about— probably thought it wouldn't happen. My heart goes out to all of the innocent victims of this horrible and vicious attack of terrorism."

"We will strive now very hard to save as many people as possible. And to send a message that the City of New York and the United States of America is much stronger than any group of barbaric terrorists. That our democracy, that our rule of law, that our strength and our willingness to defend ourselves will ultimately prevail."

Later that day, his remarks were designed to reassure every New Yorker that the city had a bright future. "New York is still here," he said. "We've undergone tremendous losses, but New York is going to be here tomorrow morning and this is the way of life that people want throughout the world."

The way Giuliani handled the crisis brought him accolades all around. Queen Elizabeth conferred honorary knighthood on him. *Saturday Night Live*, the city's offbeat late-night comedy show, pressed him into service as a host. Others spoke of him as America's Winston Churchill. It was hard to believe that this was the same Giuliani who had received so much flak from the media for his bunker mentality, his messy personal life, and what some claimed was a laissez-faire attitude toward police brutality. Even his critics spoke admiringly of the leadership he provided in the aftermath of September 11th.

In a pinch, Giuliani had come through for his city.

He was born in 1944 to Italian immigrant parents in Brooklyn. His grandfather had owned a cigar shop, but chose to give up the business rather than pay the Mafia a "protection" fee. The young Giuliani seemed to have politics in his blood. He was voted class politician at his high school even though he hadn't been elected to any school position. But he did work for the election of JFK during those high school years and prided himself on being a strong liberal Democrat.

Giuliani graduated magna cum laude from New York University Law School and worked as an assistant attorney for the Southern District of New York, before moving to Washington, DC, where he established himself as a brilliant cross-examiner. He was appointed associate deputy attorney general during the Ford administration. Shortly afterward, he switched his party affiliation to Republican.

Giuliani returned to private practice in New York three years later. He was eventually appointed associate attorney general under the Reagan administration. But the role that was to win him the most notice was U.S. attorney for the Southern District of New York. In that job, he took on organized crime with a vengeance.

"We want people to hear that this city is the most aggressive in fighting against organized crime," he said at the time. He did not forget what had happened to his grandfather, nor his grandfather's hatred of the mob. Now it was payback time.

"My father saw them as bullies, as people who had to band together in order to have the courage to do things," wrote Giuliani in 1987.

In 1989 Giuliani made his first bid for mayor, but David Dinkins beat him by a slim margin. Giuliani ran successfully in 1993, becoming the first Republican mayor of New York City in 20 years.

During his tenure, the crime rate dropped 30 percent. The murder rate was at its lowest level in 25 years. The welfare rolls were trimmed by 100,000. Tourism flourished. But his methods drew serious criticism. He was accused of directing the police force as if it were a personal army, and of looking the other way at accusations of police abuses and brutality. He was also accused of fueling racial tensions and dividing the city into factions. If that weren't enough, as his term came to an end, his personal life was in shambles. News of his affair surfaced. Giuliani's relationship with his wife of 17 years became so acrimonious, he moved out of Gracie Mansion.

Despite all this, he had his eyes set on a Congressional seat—the one Hillary Clinton ultimately landed. Giuliani had served as mayor for as long as the law allows, and he wanted to remain in public office. But then a bout with prostate cancer forced him to withdraw from the race.

Fortunately, the cancer went into remission. His divorce came through and things seemed to be quieting down.

Then came September 11th.

In the days that followed, Giuliani showed what consummate leader-ship is. He led the grim tours through Ground Zero, walking through the area himself at least once each day so he could encourage—and honor—the rescue workers.

When he appeared on *Saturday Night Live*, he told the audience, "Good evening. Since September 11th, many people have called New York a city of heroes. Well, these are the heroes."

Then he indicated the uniformed police and firefighters in the audience. He praised them as "brave men and women."

He was also the first to remind people that events could have been worse.

"The thing I don't think people have focused on is that they saved 25,000 people in there," said Giuliani. "There were people on the World Trade Center's 104th floor who walked all the way down."

Post-disaster management was so absorbing that Giuliani didn't want to give it up. When talk surfaced that he was seeking ways to remain in office, his opponents were quick to accuse him of opportunism. He defended himself. He said it was tough for him to see the city he had loved and served for so long in this kind of crisis. "I couldn't walk away from it," he said.

Giuliani's legacy is set as the mayor who proved himself up to the job during the city's most devastating crisis. He believes the city will be stronger for having survived it, too.

Quoting Winston Churchill in one of his many speeches, he said, "Our hearts are broken, but they are beating, and they are beating stronger than ever."

# REMEMBERING THOSE KILLED IN THE LINE OF DUTY

"You're all my heroes. You have been from the time I was a little boy, and from the day that I became the mayor of New York City."
—*Mayor Rudy Giuliani in his Sept. 16 address to the New York Fire Department*

"You are all heroes and I have never been prouder to be a member of the NYPD than I am right now. God bless you, God bless America, God bless the NYPD."
—*Police Commissioner Bernard Kerik, speaking to his fellow officers shortly after the terrorist attacks*

If you were to ask them, any one of them, they would shrug and say, "It's just my job. I get paid to do it." Yet, it takes a very special person to choose work that serves the public, work that routinely exposes an employee to danger in the performance of his duties. A very special person indeed.

We take their bravery and sacrifices for granted. Yet, if September 11th taught us anything, it was to be grateful for the generosity of all of the police officers, firefighters, paramedics and emergency medical technicians who serve us each day; grateful for their daily acts of heroism that often go unnoticed; and grateful for their willingness to do whatever is necessary to preserve lives and uphold the law.

No words can adequately express the nation's gratitude to all the public servants who risked their lives in the performance of their duties on September 11th. That includes all of the rescue workers at the Pentagon. Fortunately, none of the rescuers in Arlington, VA, died that day. In New York, it was a very different story.

Three hundred and forty-one New York City firefighters, their two paramedics, 23 New York Police Department officers and 37 Port Authority Police officers and commanders laid down their lives for others. For their great and loving sacrifice, their awesome bravery, we can never be thankful enough. May they continue to inspire us even as the memory of that day fades.

Made in the USA
Charleston, SC
27 May 2015